Mediæval Reactions to the Encounter between Faith and Reason

The Aquinas Lecture, 1995

Mediæval Reactions
to the
Encounter
between
Faith and Reason

Under the auspices of the
Wisconsin-Alpha of Phi Sigma Tau

by

JOHN F. WIPPEL

Marquette University Press
Milwaukee
1995

Library of Congress Catalog Card Number: 94-74397

ISBN 0-87462-162-3

Copyright © 1994

Marquette University Press

Published in the United States of America

Prefatory

The Wisconsin-Alpha Chapter of Phi Sigma Tau, the National Honor Society for Philosophy at Marquette University, each year invites a scholar to deliver a lecture in honor of St. Thomas Aquinas.

The 1995 Aquinas Lecture, *Mediæval Reactions to the Encounter between Faith and Reason*, was delivered in the Tony and Lucille Weasler Auditorium on Sunday, February 26, 1995, by Monsignor John F. Wippel, Ordinary Professor of Philosophy in the School of Philosophy and Academic Vice-President of The Catholic University of America.

Born in Pomeroy, Ohio, John Wippel began his seminary training at St. John Vianney Seminary in Steubenville, Ohio and completed his undergraduate work at The Catholic University of America where he also earned an M.A. in Philosophy and a Licentiate in Sacred Theology. After ordination in 1960 he taught for one year at The Catholic University of America and then pursued doctoral studies at the University of Louvain which awarded him the Ph.D. in 1965. He also holds the post-doctoral degree of *Maître-Agrégé de l'Ecole Saint Thomas d'Aquin* from Louvain-la-Neuve which he received in 1981. He resumed teaching at The Catholic University of America in 1963 and became Ordinary Professor in 1972. Since June of 1989 he has been Academic Vice-President of the University.

Monsignor Wippel received the Cardinal Mercier prize from the University of Louvain in 1981 for his book, *The Metaphysical Thought of Godfrey of Fontaines*. He is also the author of *Metaphysical Themes in Thomas Aquinas* (1984). He is coeditor and coauthor of *Medieval Philosophy: From St. Augustine to Nicholas of Cusa* (1969); he is editor of *Studies in Medieval Philosophy* (1987) and author of the chapter in that volume on "Thomas Aquinas and Participation." He is coauthor of *Les questions disputées et les questions quodlibétiques dans les facultés de théologie, de droit et de médecine* (1985), having contributed Part II of that volume, "Quodlibetal Questions, Chiefly in Theology Faculties." He has translated *Boethius of Dacia: On the Supreme Good, On the Eternity of the World, On Dreams* (1987).

Besides his books, Msgr. Wippel is the author of over fifty articles in journals and in encyclopedias and chapters in books on mediæval philosophy. Some of his most recent articles bear the following titles: "Godfrey of Fontaines: Divine Power and the Principle of Noncontradiction," "Individuation in James of Viterbo," "Thomas Aquinas on What Philosophers Can Know about God," "Thomas of Sutton on Divine Knowledge of Future Contingents," "The Latin Avicenna as a Source for Thomas Aquinas's Metaphysics," and "Truth in Thomas Aquinas."

To Msgr. John F. Wippel's distinguished list of publications, Phi Sigma Tau is pleased to add: *Mediæval Reactions to the Encounter between Faith and Reason*.

MEDIÆVAL REACTIONS
TO THE
ENCOUNTER
BETWEEN
FAITH AND REASON

by

JOHN F. WIPPEL

Mediæval Reactions to the Encounter between Faith and Reason

John F. Wippel

Introduction

In order to introduce this topic I would like to turn to the Prologue of Bishop Stephen Tempier's well known condemnation of 219 propositions issued March 7, 1277, at Paris.[1] However one may assess the justification for such action on the part of the Bishop, the contents of his decree point to a crisis at the University of Paris. According to the Prologue, the prohibited propositions were allegedly taught by certain members from the Arts Faculty there at that time. After denouncing these members from Arts for having exceeded the limits of their own faculty, the Bishop comments:

> So as not to appear to be asserting what they thus insinuate, however, they conceal their answers in such a way that, while wishing to avoid Scylla, they fall into Charybdis. For they say that these things are true according to philosophy but not according to the Catholic Faith,

as if there were two contrary truths, and as if the
truth of Sacred Scripture is opposed to the truth
in the sayings of the accursed pagans, of whom
it is written, 'I will destroy the wisdom of the
wise.' (I Corinthians 1:19).[2]

It is generally agreed today that no members of the
Arts Faculty of that time in fact defended a double-
truth theory, i.e., the claim that two contradictory
propositions could both be true at one and the same
time.[3] But I have cited this text for other reasons, to
show how acute the encounter between faith and
reason had become in Parisian philosophical and
theological circles by that time, and also to show
how widely received was the distinction between
what one accepts as true on the strength of divine
revelation, on the one hand, and on the strength of
unaided human reason, on the other.

I. EARLIER REACTIONS TO THE FAITH-REASON ISSUE

The distinction between faith and reason was
not an original discovery on the part of the thirteenth century, of course. It is already present in some
of the Fathers of the Church, especially so in St.
Augustine. While Augustine was interested in con-
structing what might best called a Christian wisdom
rather than any kind of separate philosophy, he was
quite familiar with and well versed in philosophical
thinking, especially in Neoplatonism. For his appreciation of the distinction between understanding or
proving something on purely rational or philosophi-

cal grounds and believing it on divine authority, one may turn to Bk II of his *De libero arbitrio*. There, in attempting to buttress the claim that God gave free will to human beings, he raises the issue of God's existence. Augustine is not content to let his partner in this dialogue, Evodius, accept God's existence solely on the grounds of religious belief. In fact, in the course of Bk II, Augustine gradually works out one of the strongest and lengthiest versions of an argument for God's existence based on eternal truths that the Western world would ever see. At the conclusion of this argument Augustine maintains that he and his dialogue partner now accept God's existence as true not only by faith, but by a sure if somewhat tenuous form of reasoning.[4]

At the same time, in this same treatise Augustine had argued that it is one thing for us to believe that God exists on the authority of Scripture. It is something else for us to know and to understand what we believe. "Unless believing is different from understanding, and unless we first believe the great and divine thing that we desire to understand, the prophet has said in vain: 'Unless you believe, you shall not understand'." As a consequence, we find in Augustine strong support for a position adopted many centuries later by St. Anselm of Canterbury— Unless you believe, you will not understand.[5]

For Augustine this admonition does not mean that he has therefore rejected the role of rational or philosophical argumentation. It does mean that if one is to be properly disposed to appreciate fully the force of such argumentation, at least in cases involving such sublime issues as God's existence, one should first believe and then seek to understand. In fact, for Augustine in Bk II of his *De libero arbitrio*, working out a conclusive argument for God's existence based on eternal truths is a good illustration of what it means to understand.

Also worth mentioning in this respect is the contribution of Boethius. In him the Latin West had a good illustration of a Christian who could and did write purely philosophical works, and who also produced some theological tractates. Even one of the latter, often referred to as his *De hebdomadibus*, is in fact highly philosophical; indeed, it is almost a work of pure philosophy. In addition to this treatise and to his logical writings and translations, his *Consolation of Philosophy* must be recognized as a significant literary and philosophical contribution to subsequent Latin thought. Hence, if he did not work out in detail a theoretical solution to the faith-reason issue, he illustrated in practice how one might be both a believing Christian and a philosophical thinker and writer and, in most of his theological tractates, how one might apply reason to the content of faith.[6]

For a more clearly recognizable continuation of the Augustinian tradition on the faith-reason issue developed in highly original fashion, one may leap forward in time to St. Anselm of Canterbury in the late tenth and early eleventh centuries. In fact, one might call him the mediæval herald of this approach—*fides quaerens intellectum* (faith seeking understanding). By Anselm's time the intellectual climate in the Latin world had changed considerably. The Carolingian revival had come and gone, and had been followed by a period of increased interest in dialectic, or in what we might call correct logical thinking and argumentation. This was owing in part to the fact that a small part of Aristotle's logical writings had been preserved in Latin translation for the largely non-Greek reading Latin West since the time of Boethius's translations of these works. This heritage included an Introduction by Porphyry to the first of Aristotle's logical works, known as the *Isagoge*, along with Aristotle's *Categories* itself and his *De interpretatione* and Boethius's independently authored logical treatises. It was only after Anselm's time that the other parts of Aristotle's logical writings were rediscovered in Boethius's translations or retranslated, in the case of the, *Posterior Analytics*, and then made available in Latin.[7]

While controversies had broken out between dialecticians and anti-dialecticians before and during Anselm's time, participants on both sides were well versed in the logic of the day, or in dialectic. One is reminded of St. Peter Damian, one of the leading anti-dialecticians, and the dialectical skill he manifests in his letter *On Divine Omnipotence*. There he examines the question whether God has the power to make past events not to have been and offers dia-

lectical arguments for each side. In fact, by appeal-
ing to the authority of faith, he pushes his case so far as
to suggest that God does indeed possess such power.[8]

Anselm himself was highly skilled in dialectic as
his writings clearly attest. While he, like Augustine,
was still interested in contributing to the development of a Christian wisdom, he penned writings that
are clearly theological and others that are more philosophical in content. For examples of the latter one
may cite his *De grammatico*, to be sure, but also his
De veritate, and *De libertate arbitrii*. As their modern translators note in referring to the latter two,
while Anselm does appeal to biblical or ecclesiastical authority in these treatises, "his manner of argument is such as to seek for rational rather than con-
fessional bases" for his conclusions.[9] And almost ev-
eryone is familiar with the interesting combination
of philosophical and theological reasoning present
in his *Monologion* of 1076, and the considerable
amount of philosophical content present in his
Proslogion of 1077-1078.[10]

While Anselm would not separate philosophy
from theology so sharply as would some thirteenth-
and fourteenth-century writers, he was deeply interested in finding convincing arguments (*rationes*)
to support or to demonstrate rationally conclusions
he had originally accepted on faith. So confident is
he of possible success in such an undertaking that
he even claims to have discovered necessary arguments (*rationes necessariae*) to support, even to dem-

onstrate, some truths which almost all other leading Christian thinkers would regard as beyond human reason's ability to prove and hence as matters of purely religious belief. Thus in his *Cur Deus Homo*, surely directed to a central religious and theological topic, he notes in the Preface that he has divided this treatise into two books. The first deals with certain objections raised by unbelievers who reject the Christian religion because they regard it as repugnant to human reason. Hence, setting aside all one's belief in Christ as if nothing were known about him, Anselm promises to prove by necessary arguments (*rationes*) that it is impossible for anyone to be saved without Christ.[11]

In Bk I, ch. 1 he writes that in replying to those who inquire about this particular problem of the Christian faith, i.e., why God became man, he is accustomed to give the rational foundation, the *rationes*, for such belief. He is now about to set down such thoughts in writing. Those Christians who have asked him to do this have made this request not in order that they might approach their faith by beginning with reason, but so that they might take delight in understanding and contemplating that which they believe, and that they might be prepared to give satisfactory answers to those who ask them for the reason for that hope which lies within them.[12]

To me this means that for Anselm the Augustinian call to believe first and then to seek to understand continues to hold. For Anselm the dialectician, to find necessary reasons for that which one already believes is part of the task of an enlightened faith. But Anselm also recognizes here and even more so in his *Proslogion* that rational argumentation can also be effective in dealing with an unbeliever and in enabling such a person to move from unbelief to belief. This more apologetical appeal to reason can and, in the case of the *Proslogion's* argumentation for God's existence and its derivation of the divine attributes, surely does lead to major contributions to mediæval philosophical thought by Anselm.[13]

II. The High Middle Ages

1: *The New Philosophical Sources.*

Before we turn to the thirteenth-century encounter between faith and reason, a word should be said about the new philosophical sources that had become available by that time. Reference has already been made to the Boethian translations of Aristotle's *Categories* and *De interpretatione* and his translation of Porphyry's *Isagoge* which remained known to Western thinkers during the following centuries. These works constituted what was often referred to as the Old Logic (*Logica vetus*) and were also used in Anselm's time. Not too long thereafter, more or less paralleling the end of Peter Abelard's career, the remaining works from Aristotle's logical corpus, known as the New Logic (*Logica nova*) again became available in Latin translation.[14]

Whether any of these works (*Logica nova*) were already available in time for Abelard to employ them effectively, especially the *Prior* and *Posterior Analytics*, is highly unlikely.[15] Nonetheless, their absence did not prevent Abelard from making significant contributions to the development of logic (dialectic). And we should also note, if only in passing, that Abelard himself is another good example of a mediæval writer who could produce purely philosophical works (in logic), and who would eventually turn his attention to theological topics as well, if only to run counter to ecclesiastical authority in some of his theological endeavors.

Especially interesting efforts to come to terms with the faith-reason issue are to be found in two of his works, his *Dialogue between a Philosopher, a Jew, and a Christian*, and his treatise on Ethics, *Scito Teipsum*. The first work is difficult for us to interpret both because of its unfinished nature, and because it is sometimes not easy to determine whether Abelard himself holds the views he assigns there to the Philosopher or to the Christian. In the second part of the *Dialogue*, where the conversation is between the Philosopher and the Christian, the emphasis shifts to the meeting between pagan philosophical and Christian views on morality. This great interest in ethical problems is central to Abelard's *Scito Teipsum*, though there the perspective is decidedly more theological.[16]

But in neither of these works nor, for that matter, in his other strictly theological works, does Abelard work out a fully satisfying or consistent solution to the faith-reason issue. Nonetheless, he clearly had a high appreciation of the value of philosophical thinking and writing both in its own right and as a tool for theological reflection.[17]

Shortly after Abelard's time the treasury of philosophical literature of non-Christian origins available in Latin translation became much greater. Thus Aristotle's other logical writings, known as the *Logica nova*, soon became available, and owing to this translation activity both from Arabic into Latin and from Greek into Latin, by the year 1200 or thereabouts the major part of the Stagirite's writings were accessible in whole or at least in part in Latin translation. Along with these, Latin translations of important Arabic originals by thinkers such as Al-Kindi, Al-Farabi, Avicenna, Algazel, Averroes and Moses Maimonides also became available to Christian thinkers during the twelfth and thirteenth centuries together with commentaries on Aristotle by classical commentators such as Alexander, Simplicius, Themistius, Ammonius, and John Philoponus, and a number of other pseudo-Aristotelian and related works.[18]

As more and more of these previously unknown philosophical sources began circulating in the West, it was inevitable that Christian thinkers would have to react to and absorb this new learning. And precisely because so much of it was purely philosophical, they would also have to reflect more deeply about the appropriate stance Christian thinkers should take on the faith-reason issue. As is well known, the path was not always smooth.

2: *Early Ecclesiastical Reactions.*

Already in the year 1210 a council was held at Paris for the Bishops of the ecclesiastical province of Sens. The views of two individuals—David of Dinant and Amalric of Bène—were singled out for condemnation, and a prohibition was issued under penalty of excommunication against "reading" the books of Aristotle on natural philosophy or the Commentaries on the same at the newly founded University of Paris. New statutes for the Faculty of Arts at the University were promulgated in 1215 by Robert of Courçon (formerly a theology professor at Paris and then Papal Legate). After requiring that Masters in Arts should read Aristotle's books on both the old and new logic, and after mentioning reading Aristotle's *Ethics* and *Topics*, Bk 4, the statutes prohibited reading Aristotle's *Metaphysics* and books on "natural philosophy" as well as *Summae* of the same. "Reading" should be taken in these texts in the sense of lecturing, and the Commentaries and *Summae* in question were probably Avicenna's paraphrases. Private consultation was not prohibited, nor were Masters in Theology prevented from using them.[19]

In a letter to the Masters of Theology at Paris of July 7, 1228, Pope Gregory IX warned them against relying unduly on philosophy and profane novelties in their teaching of theology. Evidently many of them were now using the new philosophical sources. And another letter from the Pope on April 13, 1231, *Parens scientiarum Parisius,* aimed at ending a great University strike of some two years duration, also directed that Masters of Arts at Paris should not use the previously prohibited *libri naturales* until they had been examined and purged from all suspicion of error. Ten days later, in a letter of April 23, the Pope appointed a three-man commission to examine Aristotle's *libri naturales.* The probable chairman of the commission, William of Auxerre, died in Rome in November 1231, and this may explain why the commission never carried out its task. The fact that it would have been practically impossible to purge Aristotle's writings may have been another reason.[20]

So far as we can determine, the prohibition against lecturing on these works was observed in the main in the Arts Faculty until at least ca. 1240. This is reflected in the surviving works produced by these Masters until that time, which concentrate heavily on logic and ethics rather than on metaphysics and natural philosophy, and some of which also take care to distinguish between philosophy and theology. But Roger Bacon clearly did lecture on the *libri naturales* during his time as a Master in Arts at Paris, i.e., ca. 1245. And by the year 1250 or thereabouts, Aristotle was securely established both in Arts and in Theology at Paris, so much so, in fact that the 1255 statutes for the Arts Faculty required reading all of the known works of Aristotle. Hence by that time we can already speak of a Latin Aristotelianism in both of these faculties at Paris, though in each case we are dealing with versions of Aristotle which are heavily colored by Neoplatonic and Avicennian elements.[21]

The cause of Aristotle was greatly helped by Albert the Great who taught at Paris from 1240 or 1243 as a Bachelor and then as a Master in Theology until he moved to Cologne in 1248. Aristotle's cause was also significantly advanced by Thomas Aquinas, who followed Albert to Cologne in 1248 but returned to Paris as a Bachelor and then as a Master in Theology from 1252 until 1259, and who would again serve as *Magister regens* in Theology there from 1269 until 1272. Albert's reputation was immense and in addition to his many theological writings, he would eventually produce an extensive list of commentaries or paraphrases on Aristotle's works.[22]

Aquinas's contributions to the spread of Aristotle are so well known that I will not detail them here, though I will return below to his views on the faith-reason issue. Suffice it to say that from the very beginning of his literary career he was quite familiar with and very positively disposed toward the works of the philosophers while developing his personal philosophical and theological thought. Albert's influence in developing this spirit in the young Aquinas should not be overlooked. Thomas, too, would eventually produce a series of highly regarded literal commentaries on many of Aristotle's works.[23]

Many Latin thinkers recognized that there was much of value in the writings of Aristotle and his Greek commentators and in Arabic originals penned by Al-Kindi, Al-Farabi, Avicenna, Algazel, Averroes, and Moses Maimonides. But it also came to be rec-

ognized, if only gradually in some cases as with
Averroes's Long Commentary on the *De anima*, that
some of their views—even many in certain cases—
were at odds with orthodox Christian belief.[24]

3: *Radical Aristotelianism.*

Also worth mentioning was the development of
the Faculty of Arts at Paris as a center for philosophical studies by the 1260s and 1270s, if not earlier.
This development, along with the circumstances already mentioned above, set the stage for the appearance of another kind of Latin Aristotelianism in that
faculty in the 1260s which would provoke considerable alarm in various quarters, and which would
eventually lead to the prohibition of 13 propositions
by Bishop Stephen Tempier of Paris in 1270, and
then of 219 articles in 1277. Sometimes referred to
as Latin Averroism, this movement in the Arts Faculty was much broader than that and can be better
described as Heterodox Aristotelianism, as Van
Steenberghen preferred, or as Radical Aristotelianism, as I prefer to do.[25]

While relatively little is known about the origins of
this movement in the Arts Faculty prior to the Condemnation of 1270, cooperative research in recent decades has
shed more light on these events.[26] For instance, it has long
been known that St. Bonaventure attacked some of the
views defended by adherents of this movement in his Lenten
Conferences of 1267 and 1268.[27]

More recently, Ignatius Brady has made known and edited some questions of the Franciscan Master, William of Baglione, which date from 1266-1267, and which address in detail certain positions condemned by Tempier in 1270, especially those having to do with numerical unity of the possible intellect, the denial that this individual human being can be said to understand, and the theological issue concerning whether the separated soul suffers from fire. William's discussion of unicity of the possible intellect, by the way, indicates that he already had a first-hand knowledge of Averroes's Commentary on the *De anima*. This issue was crucial, of course, because if distinct intellective and spiritual powers are not present in different individual human beings, the possibility of personal survival after death is undercut.[28]

In any event, in December of 1270, Bishop Tempier condemned 13 propositions and excommunicated all who "shall have taught or asserted them knowingly." At least four of these are found in works by Siger of Brabant from the Arts Faculty which have been dated prior to 1270: (1) that the intellect for all human beings is numerically one and the same; (5) that the world is eternal; (6) that there never was a first human being (*homo*); (8) that the separated soul cannot suffer from corporeal fire in the afterlife.[29]

These views appear in Siger's *Quaestiones in tertium de anima* and in his *Quaestio utrum haec sit vera: homo sit animal....* Of these condemned propositions, only the first is uniquely defended by Averroes.[30] Closely related to it in the eyes of a Thomas Aquinas is the position defended by condemned proposition 2—that it is false or improper to say: a (meaning this individual) human being understands. (This would be an extreme version of the Averroistic view that only one separate possible intellect thinks in individual human beings). Personal immortality is explicitly denied by proposition 7. For Aquinas, both of these views would follow from Siger's defense of unicity of the possible intellect, even though neither is explicitly defended in so many words in Siger's surviving writings.[31]

Other prohibited propositions would subject human beings to sheer necessity and thereby undercut freedom of choice (3, 4), or reduce the will to a purely passive power moved necessarily by the desired object (9), or reject God's knowledge of individuals (10) or of things other than himself (11) or his providence (12), or Christian belief in the resurrection of the body (13).[32]

In the year 1270 Thomas Aquinas produced his *De unitate intellectus (contra Averroistas)*, attacking not only Averroes but his Latin followers, presumably Siger of Brabant above all others. Aquinas challenged unicity of the intellect both as a defensible reading of Aristotle and on purely philosophical grounds. The appearance of the term "Averroists" in the title in some ancient manuscripts undoubtedly did much to introduce this expression into later usage. Yet for Thomas the particular Averroistic position at issue was unicity of the possible intellect.[33] As for Siger of Brabant, Thomas's intervention, along with Bishop Stephen's Condemnation of 1270, seems to have had a moderating effect on his subsequent discussions of unicity of the intellect and on other points as well, as will be seen below. Such development did not save him, along with Boethius of Dacia, from becoming major targets of Tempier's much more sweeping condemnation in March 1277.

Indeed, during the 1270s various events indicate that the Condemnation of 1270 had not destroyed the Radical Aristotelian movement in the Faculty of Arts. For instance, St. Bonaventure's *Collationes in Hexaëmeron* of 1273 point to continuing concern on his part about certain errors of Aristotle and other "Arab" philosophers. Bonaventure maintains that Aristotle's rejection of divine exemplar causality was at the root of many of his other shortcomings in metaphysics, such as the absence of a doctrine of divine knowledge of individuals, divine providence, and divine foreknowledge of contingents, the "Arabs'" introduction of a doctrine of necessitating fate, and Aristotle's omission of a theory of reward and punishment in the life to come. Bonaventure also singles out Aristotle's seeming defense of an eternal world and unicity of the intellect as this is attributed to Aristotle by Averroes.[34]

Giles of Rome's *Errores Philosophorum*, dated by its modern editor between 1268 and 1274, is added evidence of concern about the views of Aristotle, Averroes, Avicenna, Algazel, Al-Kindi, and Maimonides.[35] And if one agrees with Van Steenberghen that Giles of Lessine's letter to Albert the Great falls after 1270, it also points to continuing concern in the 1270s about certain heterodox positions being advanced by leading members in Arts of that time (*qui in philosophia maiores reputantur*). Thirteen of the fifteen propositions listed by Giles are identical with the thirteen condemned by Tempier in 1270.[36] Giles of Rome's *De plurificatione intellectus possibilis* seems to date from the mid 1270s. It is yet another witness to ongoing concern about the issue of unicity of the human possible intellect. Certain anonymous Commentaries on Aristotle's *De anima* and *Physics* dating from the 1270s also contain views which would be addressed in the Condemnation of 1277.[37]

4: *The Condemnation of 1277.*

It is not all that surprising, therefore, that Pope John XXI, himself a former Master in Arts at Paris and better known to us as Peter of Spain, would write to Stephen Tempier on January 18, 1277, and ask him to undertake an investigation about certain dangerous doctrines which were rumored to be circulating at the University. The Bishop was to determine by whom and where such errors were being propagated and to report his findings back to the Pope as soon as possible. Instead, as is well known,

Stephen assembled a commission of sixteen theologians, including Henry of Ghent, and apparently consulted some additional personal advisers as well. In short order a list of 219 propositions was drawn up. Without reporting back to the Pope before acting, he issued his sweeping condemnation on March 7, 1277, ironically three years to the day after the death of Thomas Aquinas in 1274.[38]

While this list is much broader in range than the 13 propositions condemned in 1270, the concerns addressed there reappear, along with many more. Considerable study has been devoted to this event beginning especially in 1977 on the occasion of its 700th anniversary, and continuing down to the present time. Important books have been published by R. Hissette, L. Bianchi, and K. Flasch, along with many other article-length studies or book chapters.[39] Yet puzzles remain.

For instance, while many of the condemned propositions clearly undermine orthodox Christian teaching whether measured by that day's standards or by those of today, other propositions do not. Thus some twenty years later, Godfrey of Fontaines, an esteemed member of the Theology faculty, would publicly defend Thomas Aquinas for having been touched by the prohibition of 1277 and would conclude that the then Bishop of Paris should at least suspend the condemnation of those propositions which appeared to have been taught by Thomas.[40] In fact this step was not taken, but in 1325, two years after Aquinas's canonization, Stephen of Bourret, the Bishop of Paris at that time, revoked the condemnation of those articles in so far as they touched on or were asserted to touch on Aquinas's teaching.[41]

One can only conclude that on points such as these, Tempier's advisers and/or Tempier himself were so colored by their own theological positions that they easily regarded opposed views as heterodox. There was a highly conservative group within the Theology Faculty itself which was opposed to many of Aquinas's philosophical and theological positions as well as to the clearly heterodox views of the Radical Aristotelians. Moreover, a somewhat later remark by Giles of Rome makes it clear that some of the propositions were condemned not on the advice of the Masters but because of the stubbornness of a certain few. Giles may have had in mind some of Tempier's other advisers as well as Tempier himself.[42]

Even so, today we find it difficult to understand why it would have been regarded as heretical to hold that because separate intelligences lack matter, God cannot produce many intelligences within the same species (43-81), or to maintain that God cannot multiply individuals within a species without matter (42-96).[43] Also puzzling is the condemnation of certain views defended by Albert and by Thomas as well as by certain Masters in Arts concerning the presence of angels in place. Witness proposition 55-204 and the seeming incompatibility of its being condemned along with proposition 54-219, as

Godfrey of Fontaines pointed out in his Quodlibet XII, q. 5, and as even Henry of Ghent, a member of the commission of theologians as we have noted, himself recognized in his Quodlibet II, q. 9, dating from the Christmas quodlibetal session of 1277, and hence only a few months after the Condemnation of March 7.[44]

On the other hand, it is easy enough to understand why many other propositions were censured. A number of them bear on the nature of philosophy and, at least when taken at first sight and out of context, appear to do so at the expense of theology. For instance, proposition 1-40 is generally acknowledged to be directed against Boethius of Dacia's *De summo bono*. It reads: "There is no more excellent kind of life than to give oneself to philosophy." When taken out of context this condemned proposition would leave no place for the religious believer to hold that the life of the saint or the mystic or the theologian might be more excellent. But when taken in context within the treatise, it is clear that Boethius is seeking to determine, by relying on reason alone, what is the supreme good accessible to human beings. In fact, he does recognize in one passage a higher kind of happiness "which we expect in the life to come on the authority of faith." Again, proposition 2-154 states that "Only the philosophers are the wise men of this world." This appears to be directed against another treatise of Boethius, his *De aeternitate mundi*. But in that text Boethius states that the "philoso-

phers were and are the wise men of this world." The
qualifier "only" does not appear in Boethius's text.[45]

Other propositions directly challenge the value
of the Christian Law, for instance, 180-175: "That
the Christian Law impedes one from learning" and
181-174: "That fables and falsities are present in the
Christian Law as in others." Still others are directed
against the value of theology, for instance, 182-153:
"One knows nothing more when one knows theology," and 183-152: "The statements of the theologian are based on fables." But it must be acknowledged that no one has yet successfully identified with
certainty the precise source or target for any of these.[46]

A number of condemned propositions compromise God's knowledge of individuals, or his providence,
or his omnipotence.[47] Still others deny that God can
produce anything *de novo*, or more than one world, or
that he can immediately produce more than one effect, thereby recalling the Neoplatonic Avicennian
theory of mediate rather than immediate creation
through a process of necessary emanation.[48] Eternity
of separate intelligences or of the universe is defended
or implied by a number of other propositions.[49] Others have to do with unicity of the possible intellect,
while still other condemned propositions detract from
or eliminate human freedom.[50] Propositions 185-1 and
186-2 would reject Christian belief in the Trinity and
in the eternal generation of the Word.

A considerable number of the prohibited propositions deal with moral matters, such as the claim

that one should not pray (202-180), or that one should not confess one's sins except for the sake of appearances (203-179), or that simple fornication (between an unmarried man and an unmarried woman) is not a sin (205-183), or that there are no virtues other than the acquired or innate (200-177).[51] Also condemned are propositions asserting that one should not be concerned if something is said to be heretical because it is against the faith (201-16), and, curiously enough, that one should not be concerned about burying the dead (204-155).[52]

Somewhat more complex is the condemnation of the view that humility is not a virtue or a virtuous act if it leads one not to manifest that which one has and to despise and debase oneself (211-171), as well as the claim that one who is poor (deprived of material goods) cannot act well in moral matters (212-170). The remote source for the position on humility is surely Aristotle's *Nicomachean Ethics*, Bk IV, c. 3, where he discusses the great souled person and one who is unduly humble. The proximate source appears to be the first of Siger of Brabant's moral questions ("Whether humility is a virtue"), where he distinguishes two meanings of humility, one an extended and changed meaning which applies to someone who pretends to lesser good in himself than he actually has, and the other a proper meaning describing that which restricts one's appetite from tending to extremely arduous goods which are beyond him according to right reason. According to Siger the former is not a virtue but the latter, along with greatness of soul, is.[53]

The remote source for the proposition requiring material goods for right moral action also appears to be Aristotle's *Ethics*, Bk X, c. 8, but the proximate source may be an anonymous commentary on the *De anima* edited by M. Giele. There the author sums up Aristotle's position by citing him as holding: "Blessed are those who are well provided with external goods," and contrasts this with the Christian view: "Blessed are the poor in spirit, for theirs is the kingdom of heaven."[54]

Also interesting is the condemnation of the statement that death is the end of things to be feared (213-178), especially so if R.–A. Gauthier is correct in thinking that it was taken from a *Tabula libri Ethicorum* (an alphabetical catalog of positions) drawn up from the *Nicomachean Ethics* and Albert's Commentary on it under Thomas Aquinas's direction by a secretary ca. 1270.[55]

Many scholars have been struck by the haphazard way in which the various propositions were organized in the original list, and there have been both medieval and modern efforts to impose greater order and organization upon them. But K. Flasch has recently come to the defense of the original ordering. On the other hand, L. Bianchi has offered an interesting and plausible explanation for the apparent lack of overall order and organization. Different parts, he proposes, were drawn up on separate rolls by different members of the Commission, and then simply attached to one another in succession.[56] In any event, inconsistencies appear within the final list, and on at least some occasions, mutually exclusive propositions are condemned, as Godfrey of Fontaines pointed out long ago.[57]

Another puzzle has to do with the intended direct targets of the condemnation. Apart from two books which are identified in the Prologue, neither the titles nor the authors of the works from which the propositions were drawn are explicitly named.[58] Both internal evidence and early manuscript testimony indicate that Siger of Brabant and Boethius of Dacia were primary targets.[59]

Hissette has concluded from his careful investigation that of the 219 articles, 30 appear to envision directly Siger of Brabant, and 13 directly target Boethius of Dacia. He has also identified 14 others as directed against anonymous writings from the Arts Faculty, recently edited by Delhaye, Giele, and Zimmermann.[60] He thinks it probable that 14 more were aimed at Siger, three more at Boethius, and four at two of the anonymous works just mentioned. For 72 others he can only offer plausible hypotheses as to the identity of their intended targets, and for another 68 written sources remained unidentified.[61]

A. de Libera has focussed his attention on those propositions having to do with moral matters and, noting the difficulty of finding written sources authored by members of the Arts Faculty for many

of them, has suggested that some were not in fact
defended by Masters of Arts at the time, but were
rather projections by Tempier and/or his advisers
about dangerous views that could and eventually did
arise.[62] To some, myself included, this suggestion may
seem a bit extreme, but the absence of written sources
for a fairly large number of the condemned propositions must be acknowledged. One can only speculate
about sources from that time which have not survived,
and about others which are yet to be identified.

Also controverted today is the question as to
what extent Thomas Aquinas was directly targeted
by Tempier and his advisers. Many scholars and some
mediæval writers have noted the presence of
Aquinas's views among the condemned propositions
and have concluded that he was indeed directly targeted.[63] Hissette has stressed Tempier's statement in
the Prologue to the effect that these errors were circulating in the Faculty of Arts. Hence, while he acknowledges that a number of them do indeed express
positions defended by Aquinas, Hissette argues that in
most of these cases similar positions can be found in
the writings of Masters in Arts of that time. Therefore
the latter, not Thomas Aquinas, should be regarded as
the primary and direct targets of the prohibition.[64]

Some other interpreters, myself included, think
that Tempier and his advisers knew quite well when
they were condemning a view defended by Aquinas.
To single out perhaps the most distinguished theologian on the Commission, Henry of Ghent, he was

quite familiar with Aquinas's views on many of the disputed points. Therefore, to say that, in condemning a position defended both by a Master of Arts and by Aquinas, members of the Commission and Tempier were directly envisioning only the former appears to me to be somewhat forced, what one might call a distinction without a difference. In my opinion, Tempier and his censors were perfectly willing to include Aquinas's views in their list when they judged it appropriate.[65]

In connection with this, however, it is interesting to note that another Belgian scholar, R. Wielockx, has recently discovered and edited an intriguing set of propositions which were drawn up by Giles of Rome in defense of his own views at about the same time, i.e., in March 1277, but after the Condemnation of March 7. According to Wielockx's historical reconstruction, these resulted from a separate inquiry conducted by the theologians against Giles and, because of his refusal to retract, he was exiled from the Theology Faculty at Paris until 1285 when the Pope's intervention resulted in his reinstatement.[66]

Moreover, though perhaps with somewhat less compelling evidence, Wielockx has also concluded that still another inquiry by the Masters of Theology had been initiated by Tempier against Aquinas himself. If so, this might explain why one of Thomas's most contested theories, his defense of unicity of substantial form in human beings, was not included in Tempier's list of March 7, even though it would be

included in another much shorter list condemned
by Archbishop Robert Kilwardby at Oxford a few
days later (March 18, 1277), and would again be
condemned in 1284 and 1286 by Kilwardby's successor as Archbishop of Canterbury, John Pecham.
According to Wielockx's reconstruction, Tempier's process against Aquinas did not come to term because of
instructions he received from Cardinals in the Roman
Curia during the vacancy in the papal see caused by
the death of Pope John XXI on May 20, 1277.[67]

Rather than spend more time now on official
ecclesiastical reactions to Radical Aristotelianism and
this part of the faith-reason encounter in thirteenth-
century Paris, I would like to turn to the views on
faith and reason of three principal figures in the
events just recounted—Thomas Aquinas, Siger of
Brabant and Boethius of Dacia.

III. THEORETICAL SOLUTIONS TO THE FAITH-REASON ISSUE

1: *Thomas Aquinas.*

As is well known, Aquinas defended a fundamental
harmony between faith and reason. One may consult the
first question of his *Summa theologiae*, or Bk I, cc. 4-7 of
his *Summa contra gentiles*. But perhaps nowhere else in his
writings is this brought out so clearly as in q. 2, a. 3 of his
somewhat earlier Commentary on the *De Trinitate* of
Boethius. There Thomas is defending the appropriateness

of using philosophical argumentation and authorities in the course of one's theologizing. The gifts of grace are added to nature, he writes, not so as to destroy nature but so as to perfect it. Hence the light of faith, which is given to us as a grace, does not destroy the light of natural reason which is also given to us by God. While the natural light of reason is of itself insufficient to discover those things that can be discovered only through faith, it is impossible for those things given to us by God through faith to be contrary to those which are instilled in us by nature. Otherwise, one or the other would have to be false. (Understood here, of course, is the assumption that two contradictory propositions cannot both be true at one and the same time.) And, continues Thomas, since both of these come to us from God, God himself would then be the author of falsity, something which must be rejected as impossible. Aquinas also acknowledges that by the light of natural reason certain imitations or similitudes may be discovered for those truths which are made known to us only through faith.[68]

So far Aquinas has been comparing the light of reason with the light of faith. Now he applies his thinking to theology (*sacra doctrina*) and to philosophy. Just as sacred teaching is grounded on the light of faith, philosophy is based on the natural light of reason. Therefore, it is impossible for those things which pertain to philosophy to be contrary to those which belong to faith, even though they fall short of them.[69]

One might ask, of course, especially in light of the events which would transpire at Paris soon after Thomas had written this treatise: What happens

when the findings of philosophers contradict the
teaching of faith? Thomas's serene reply is that if
anything is found in the sayings of the philosophers
which is contrary to faith, this is not philosophy but
rather an abuse of philosophy following from some
deficiency on the side of reason. Hence it will be
possible by using philosophical principles either to
reject an argument of this kind out of hand by showing that it is impossible, or at least by showing that
it is not necessary.[70]

Thomas must make this distinction if he is to avoid
falling into a kind of rationalism that would enable us
to demonstrate revealed mysteries, i.e., truths which
can be discovered only through faith. In Thomas's own
words: "Just as those things which are proper to faith
cannot be demonstratively proved, so certain things
contrary to them cannot be demonstrated to be false,
but they can be shown not to be necessary."[71]

Thomas sums this up by noting that one may
use philosophy in one's theologizing in three ways:
(1) to demonstrate certain preambles of faith, such
as those things which can be proved by natural argumentation about God, for example, that God exists, that God is one, and other things of this kind
concerning God or creatures which are proved in
philosophy and presupposed by faith; (2) to manifest mysteries of faith by certain likenesses, as Augustine often does in his *De Trinitate*; (3) to resist
attacks against the faith in the two ways just mentioned, i.e., by showing that they are false or, at least,

that they are not demonstrated.[72] As he makes clear on other occasions, e.g., in *Summa contra gentiles* I, c. 4, if there are certain truths about God which natural reason can discover, such as his existence or unity, such knowledge is not easily gained by philosophical inquiry. Consequently, Thomas also argues that it was very fitting for God to have revealed such truths to us.[73]

In light of such a position we can readily appreciate how little patience Thomas would have had with any real or even any apparent double-truth theory. Hence we can understand something of the vehemence with which he writes near the end of his *De unitate intellectus* against his unnamed Christian adversary who would defend unicity of the possible intellect. "Even more serious is what he says thereafter: 'By reason I conclude necessarily that the intellect is numerically one, but I firmly hold the opposite on faith'."[74]

Thomas faults his opponent—Siger of Brabant presumably—for thinking that faith deals with things whose contraries can be demonstrated necessarily. For Thomas only a necessary truth can be demonstrated necessarily, and its opposite is false and impossible. Indeed, in this treatise Thomas had argued against unicity of the possible intellect both on historical grounds—it is an incorrect reading of Aristotle— and on purely philosophical grounds. He had shown to his own satisfaction that the Averroistic position is both false and impossible. His Christian opponent's position would imply that faith deals with the false and the impossible, something which not even God could bring to pass. Such a position, writes Thomas, "the faithful cannot bear to hear!"[75]

And he concludes his treatise by laying down a personal challenge to Siger: "If anyone who glories in a falsely named science wishes to say anything against what we have written, let him not speak in corners nor before boys who do not know how to judge about such difficult matters: but let him respond in writing against this treatise, if he dares; and he will find not only myself, who am the least among others, but many other zealous defenders (*zelatores*) of truth by whom his error will be resisted or his ignorance remedied."[76]

Throughout his career Aquinas would remain true to his conviction that there should ultimately be harmony between faith and reason and hence, when they both are correctly practiced, between theology and philosophy. Interestingly enough, it is in this same early work, his Commentary on the *De Trinitate* of Boethius, that he works out in Question 5 his most detailed discussion of the distinctions between and the subjects of the three theoretical sciences, natural philosophy, mathematics, and metaphysics. Without pausing here to enter into a long discussion of whether he was a theologian or a philosopher or perhaps a Christian philosopher, I would only repeat the position I have developed elsewhere. He was both a philosopher and a theologian since he had recognized from the beginning of his career the need to develop a sound philosophy if he was to have any chance of developing a sound theology. For us today this means that if one is interested in studying the philosophical thought of Thomas Aquinas, one can surely do so. One should take one's cue from Thomas's own presentation of the subject matter, the distinctive methodologies, and the order to be followed in the philosophical sciences, and apply this to all of his texts which have philosophical content. In doing this one must be as conscious at all times as Thomas himself was of the distinction between faith and reason, and between philosophy and theology.[77]

Although by profession Aquinas was a theologian, his contribution to philosophical thinking was enormous, and was evidently so recognized by many of his contemporaries, including members of the Arts, i.e., the Philosophy Faculty at Paris.[78] With this I would now like to turn to two of those members from the Arts Faculty and their views on the faith-reason issue, namely, Siger of Brabant and Boethius of Dacia.

2: *Siger of Brabant.*

In dealing with Siger of Brabant, I shall use two approaches. First, I shall offer a necessarily brief overview of his actual practice when he deals with sensitive issues involving faith and reason. Second, special attention will be directed to a relatively recent discovery—a brief explicit discussion by Siger of his views on the relationship between philosophy and theology (*sacra scriptura*) preserved in two of the four surviving manuscripts of his *Quaestiones in Metaphysicam.*

Reference has already been made to the fact that some of Siger's opinions were condemned by Bishop Tempier in 1270, and that his espousal of Averroes's defense of unicity of the possible intellect had been sharply attacked in that same year by Thomas Aquinas's *De unitate intellectus.* Consequently, questions of dating and relative chronology can become important in assessing Siger's views on the faith-reason issue.

Eternity of the world is one issue on which Siger's thought seems to have developed. The recent editor of his *Quaestio utrum haec sit vera* dates this work after 1268 but before 1270. In this discussion Siger asks whether the statement that a human being is an animal would be true if no human being existed. After presenting and then rejecting a number of attempts by others to resolve this issue, Siger concludes that its hypothesis—that at some point in time the human species did not exist—is intrinsically contradictory. He notes that from such an hypothesis contradictory consequences may be drawn. But if one rejects the hypothesis itself and denies that there ever was a time when the human species did not exist, one resolves the problem. This is Siger's solution, even though it clearly implies eternity of the human species.[79]

But in another work which is prior to 1270, his *Quaestiones in tertium De anima,* Siger asks whether the (separated) intellect is eternal. He notes that according to Aristotle it is eternally produced, even as is the world. He adds that while Aristotle's position on this point—eternity of the intellect—is indeed probable, it is not necessary. It is also more probable than Augustine's defense of creation and infusion of the human soul in the course of time.[80]

In subsequent writings when he deals with the eternity of the world or of separate intelligences, Siger is careful to qualify his presentation of the eternalist position in some way. Thus he presents argumentation for the eternity of the (First) Intelligence in his *Impossibilia* (ca. 1272). The Intelligence depends for its existence on the First Principle. Since the Intelligence lacks any capacity for not-existing (for the nonexistence of its cause is impossible, and so, too, is its own nonexistence), it is impossible for it to lack that relationship to its cause by reason of which it always exists. Here we would seem to have a defense of both the eternal and necessary existence of the Intelligence. But, adds Siger, we say this according to the opinion of the philosophers.[81]

So too, in discussing eternity of the world in his *De aeternitate mundi* (ca. 1272), Siger frequently qualifies his presentation of the eternalist position by noting that this is so according to the philosophers, or according to Aristotle, or by noting that he is only repeating Aristotle's opinion.[82]

He does the same in his *De anima intellectiva* of ca. 1273. He begins by observing that, in response to the request of his friends, he here proposes to establish what is to be thought about the soul, especially about the issue of its separation from bodies. He will do so by following the texts of recognized philosophers rather than by asserting anything about this on his own. On one occasion he even remarks that perhaps "The Philosopher thought differently from the truth and from that wisdom which have been handed down through revelation concerning the soul, and which cannot be proved by natural argumentation." There he adds, echoing the words of Albert the Great, that he is not now concerned with the miracles of God, since he is discussing natural things in terms of natural philosophy.[83] Farther on in ch. 5 of this same treatise he discusses the eternal existence of the intellective soul in the past, but makes it clear that here he is presenting Aristotle's position. He also takes Aristotle as holding that the eternal intellective soul is caused.[84]

In the Cambridge manuscript version of his *Quaestiones in Metaphysicam* Siger offers an interesting comment at Bk III, q. 15 (Cambridge ms. numbering), after presenting Aristotle's view that anything that is ungenerated must also be sempiternal. These arguments do not appear to be demonstrative, comments Siger, but beg the question. Moreover, this position is opposed to what we as Christians hold to be true. Nor should we seek human arguments for things which are of faith, since such things cannot be proved by argumentation. After citing Avicenna in support of the need to rely on the testimony of the prophet in matters of faith, he adds: "I believe that, just as those things which are of faith cannot be demonstrated by human reason, so too there are some human arguments for positions opposed to such things which cannot be resolved by human reason."[85]

While this passage again confirms that Siger no longer accepts as his own Aristotle's eternalist position regarding separate (ungenerated) substances, it also reveals his acknowledgment that in certain cases human reason cannot resolve arguments which may be offered against the teachings of faith. The contrast with Aquinas's position in his *De Trinitate* is striking. There Thomas had maintained that in such cases one should be able to show by using human reason either that such positions are false or at least that they are not necessarily demonstrated![86]

Closely linked with the eternalist position was the Neoplatonic theory of necessary emanation (or creation) of the universe and the axiom that from the One only one effect can be produced immediately. This theory was well known to Thomas, to Siger and to their contemporaries because its Avicennian version was available in Latin translation. As Avicenna presents it in his *Metaphysics* IX, c. 4, from God only one effect can be produced immediately, the First Intelligence. This eternally produced Intelligence eternally produces the Second Intelligence and the soul and body of the outermost heavenly sphere. This eternal process is repeated by

the Second Intelligence which produces the Third
Intelligence and the soul and body of the second
sphere, etc., resulting ultimately in the Tenth Intelligence which is our separated Agent Intellect and also
the *Dator formarum* for terrestrial beings. Coupled with
this was the view that God necessarily produces the
First Intelligence, and that the other emanations also
follow from this necessarily and eternally.[87]

As mentioned above propositions were condemned in 1277 which defended this Neoplatonic-
Avicennian view. For instance, proposition 20-53
asserts that God must produce necessarily whatever
is made by him. Proposition 28-44 states that from
the one First Agent a multiplicity of effects cannot be
produced. And proposition 33-64 maintains that the
immediate effect of the First Cause must be only one
and most like the First Cause. Aquinas had argued at
length against this position, as one would expect.[88]

In his *De necessitate et contingentia causarum*
dating from 1271-1272 Siger presents the view that
God is the immediate and necessary cause of the
First Intelligence but only the mediate cause of other
effects such as the other Intelligences, the spheres
and their motions, and things subject to generation
and corruption. He justifies this by citing the
Neoplatonic axiom that from the one simple Being
only one effect can proceed immediately. However,
on two occasions in this discussion he refers to this
as being so according to the mind of the philosophers. Hence some question remains as to whether
this was indeed his personal position.[89]

In his *Quaestiones naturales* (Lisbon), dating from 1273-1274, the sixth question asks whether many things can be caused immediately by the First Cause. Here Siger acknowledges that he cannot demonstrate this either one way or the other. He comments that Avicenna has not really proved his claim that from the First Principle only one effect can proceed immediately.[90]

Given these passages as well as a textually mutilated discussion in the Munich version of his *Quaestiones in Metaphysicam*, a number of contemporary interpreters have concluded that Siger never really accepted the theory of necessary emanation as his personal view.[91] But the fuller and recently edited version of his *Quaestiones in Metaphysicam* V, q. 11 (Cambridge ms.), probably dating around 1273 or slightly later, reveals a Siger who sets forth this theory in sympathetic terms and argues for it. Against the claim that the First Agent by acting through its intellect can produce many different effects, Siger counters that this can be the case only if there are different ideas (*rationes*) within that intellect. But within the intellect of the First Being different ideas are not present. The First Being can understand other things only by understanding one idea (*ratio*), its own essence. It will understand many other things only insofar as within itself they are one. Moreover, Siger also here maintains that prime matter is not caused immediately by the First Cause, nor even by any immaterial substance.[92]

Yet, in his still later *Commentary on the Liber de causis* (ca. 1275-1276) Siger reserves the act of creation to the First Cause alone. Thereby he in effect rules out the theory of mediate emanation or creation which is an essential part of the Avicennian theory of emanation.[93]

In sum, therefore, Siger clearly did not accept the emanation theory as his own by the time of his *Liber de causis* and probably did not do so in his earlier works. But he seems to have been strongly attracted to this position at the time of his *Quaestiones in Metaphysicam*, and hence was not fully consistent on this issue.

As already noted, Siger's best known reason for being called a Radical Aristotelian, or in this case, a Latin Averroist, is his early defense of unicity of the receiving or possible intellect in his *Quaestiones in III De anima* which, as we have seen, dates from before 1270. There in q. 1 he denies that the vegetative, sensitive, and intellective parts of the soul are rooted in one simple substance or soul.[94] In subsequent questions he argues that the intellect does not perfect the human body through its substance but only through its power, and that it is present in the body by thinking in the body and moving it. The very nature of the intellect precludes it from being multiplied individually in individual human beings.[95] It is because intelligible objects are conjoined with us taken as individual human beings that the (single) intellect is also conjoined with us. These intelligible

objects are present in each of us because of distinct
intentions which are produced by our individual
powers of imagination. This fact enables the intellect to think in numerically distinct individual human beings, but it remains one in substance and
power.[96] The agent and the possible intellects are two
powers or two parts of one separate substance. On
this final point, Siger differs from Averroes who
would make of them not one but two distinct substances.[97]

Reference has already been made to Aquinas's
devastating attack against Averroes and Siger in his
De unitate intellectus. Not all of the points that
Thomas attributes to his opponent can be found in
Siger's *Quaestiones,* but it seems clear enough that
Siger is indeed the unnamed opponent. Perhaps
Thomas was basing himself in part on oral reports,
or on other *reportationes* of Siger's lectures.[98] It is now
widely granted that Siger did respond to Aquinas's
challenge (". . . let him respond in writing against
this treatise, if he dares . . ."), but in a lost work
known to us as his *De intellectu.* We have some
knowledge of this work owing to the testimony of
the Renaissance philosopher, Agostino Nifo. Insofar as we can judge from the excerpts and references
given by Nifo, in this treatise Siger's thought on the
human intellect had developed somewhat, but in it
he still defended unicity of the possible intellect.[99]

Far more important in tracing Siger's development on this issue is his *De anima intellectiva* of ca.

1273. As we have already noted, in the Prologue to
this work Siger proposes to state here what is to be
thought about such issues according to the texts of
the proven philosophers rather than to assert anything on his own.[100]

In Ch. III, while examining in what way the
intellective soul might be regarded as the form and
perfection of the human body, he notes that "outstanding men in philosophy, Albert and Thomas,"
hold that the substance of the intellective soul is
united to the body and gives being to it, but that the
power of the intellective soul is separate from the
body because it does not use a corporeal organ in
thinking. After pointing out certain differences in
their views, Siger criticizes both of their positions
for missing Aristotle's intention and for failing to
establish their points. His representation of Aquinas's
position is somewhat curious and not fully accurate,
but this may be because he is now struggling to an-
swer Aquinas's earlier charge in his *De unitate
intellectus* that the Averroistic and Sigerian theory
cannot really enable one to say that the act of thinking can be assigned to this or that individual human
being rather than to the separate possible intellect.[101]

But in this same context Siger acknowledges that
here he himself is only seeking to determine the view
of the philosophers and, in a passage already noted,
comments that Aristotle may have held something
other than that truth and wisdom which have been
given to us through revelation. He goes on to inter-

pret Aristotle as holding that the intellective soul is separated from the body in its being, i.e., that it is a separate intellect, but that it is united with the body in its operation.[102] Interestingly also, in Ch. VI, while seeking to determine Aristotle's view concerning the separation of the soul from the body, Siger argues that according to the Stagirite, an infinity of human beings have already existed. If each of these possessed its own intellective soul, and this soul was totally separated from its body at the time of death, an infinity of intellective souls would now exist in separation from the body. Siger finds such a view unreasonable and contrary to the mind of Aristotle, who would reject such an (actual) infinity.[103]

In this same context Siger remarks that someone may counter that it is erroneous to hold that souls are not completely separated from their bodies (after death) and do not then receive reward and punishment in accord with their behavior in this life. Siger replies that, as he has said from the beginning of this treatise, his primary purpose here is not to determine the truth of the matter concerning the soul, but rather Aristotle's view concerning this.[104]

He acknowledges that philosophers who are not familiar with the works of souls totally separated from the body may not hold that they do so exist; but there is nothing to prevent there being other human beings who are naturally prophets and who do know about things which the rest of us cannot discover except by believing in the testimony of a prophet.

In other words, Siger here acknowledges that human reason can only go so far in investigating such a topic, and suggests that if one wishes to pursue this issue any further, one should turn to revelation given through a prophet. Even so, here he refers to natural prophets rather than to prophecy based on grace and revelation, perhaps again because he is writing from the philosopher's perspective rather than from that of the Christian.[105]

In Ch. VII Siger turns to the issue of numerical multiplication of the intellective soul. Once again he warns that he is examining this question only insofar as it pertains to the philosopher and can be understood by relying on human reason and experience. He is seeking to determine the mind of the philosophers in this matter rather than the truth, since he is proceeding philosophically. He adds that it is certain according to revealed truth ("that truth which cannot deceive") that intellective souls are multiplied with the multiplication of individual human bodies. In other words, now he acknowledges that in fact each individual human being has his or her individual intellective soul, but accepts this on the strength of revelation. For he also notes that certain philosophers have maintained the opposite position, and that the opposite seems to follow from the way of philosophy.[106]

However, after offering a series of arguments against numerical multiplication of intellective souls, Siger grants that powerful arguments can also be advanced for the opposite position, i.e., to show that intellective souls are multiplied numerically even as are individual human beings. Moreover, he now also finds Avicenna and Algazel defending this view, and notes that Themistius recognizes numerical multiplication of agent intellects. With much greater reason, comments Siger, would Themistius also hold that the possible intellect is multiplied numerically. In doing this he is now taking into account other "Peripatetics" whom, Aquinas had charged in his *De unitate intellectus*, Siger and his associates had ignored by relying exclusively on Averroes.[107]

Siger concludes that because of the strong arguments that can be offered for either side of this matter, and because of the difficulty of the issue, he had long been in doubt about what should be held on the strength of natural reason and what Aristotle thought concerning numerical multiplication of the intellective soul. Now, he states: "In such doubt one must adhere to the faith which surpasses all human reasoning."[108]

In sum, Siger here adopts an undecided position concerning what natural reason can establish about numerical multiplication of the intellective soul and hence (by implication) about personal survival and immortality. He also ends by expressing doubt about what Aristotle really held on this point. He now grants a role for religious belief in deciding the issue, unless, of course, one wishes to tax him with insincerity. Earlier in this century Mandonnet did exactly that, and rejected his protests of religious belief in individual intellective souls as efforts on his part to avoid censure rather than as honest expressions of his own position. On the other hand, his sincerity had been defended by others, especially F. Van Steenberghen of Louvain. Personally, I have always been inclined to take Siger's protests of personal religious orthodoxy in this treatise at face value.[109]

In any event, the relatively recent discovery and then the publication in 1972 of a long lost work by Siger, his *Quaestiones super librum de causis*, have cast new light on this issue and especially on Siger's final recorded position. In this work, dating from ca. 1275-1276, Siger defends in q. 26 the view that the intellective soul is indeed a perfection and form of the human body, but not in such a way that we can say that the intellective power is separated. Curiously enough, in adding this qualification, Siger seems to believe he is here opposing Aquinas. In his *De unitate intellectus*, c. III, Aquinas had written that the human soul is not said to be the form of the body in terms of its intellective power, since that is the act of no organ. Hence, as regards its intellective power, Aquinas holds that the soul is immaterial, i.e., receives intelligible content in an immaterial way, and that it knows itself. And in *Summa theologiae* I, q. 76, a. 1, ad 1, Aquinas explains Aristotle's reference to the intellect as "separate" as meaning that it is not the power of a corporeal organ.[110]

Siger takes exception to this and argues that the intellective soul is the form and perfection of the body, but not in such fashion that its power is separate; rather its very substance is the act and perfection of matter and so too is its power, he maintains. But he also asserts that the intellective soul perfects the body in such fashion that it also subsists in its own right and does not depend upon matter for its existence. In granting that the intellective soul is a perfection and form of the body, and yet that it subsists in its own right, his agreement with Aquinas is much greater than his difference.[111]

Even more important is his discussion in q. 27. There he explicitly rejects the Averroistic denial that the intellect is multiplied numerically in individual human beings. He now finds that view both heretical and irrational in itself. A major part of his argument rests on the claim that if there were only one intellect for all human beings, when that intellect was united with one body or one matter as its form, it could not simultaneously be united with other bodies and matters. For it could not simultaneously think of different objects and be actually perfected by different intelligible species at one and the same time. Yet we know from experience that different individual human beings do constantly think of different objects at one and the same time. Hence the intellect must be multiplied numerically.[112]

Here we seem to have Siger's implicit acknowledgment of the justice of another of Aquinas's charges in his *De unitate intellectus* against the Averroistic position, namely, that it cannot really account for the fact that a number of different individual human beings can really think of different things at one and the same time. Of course Aquinas was also heavily moved by the testimony of consciousness and the absence of any awareness on our part that some separate intellect is really thinking in us when we are aware that we are thinking.[113]

In sum, Siger has now moved very far from his pre-1270 view concerning the intellect and is indeed defending a perfectly orthodox position when viewed from the religious side. Moreover, he has also moved beyond the hesitancy he expressed in his *De anima intellectiva* concerning what human reason can determine on this topic, even though his hesitancy about what Aristotle really held on the matter remains. Hence, as regards unicity of the intellect, had he been judged solely in light of his *Quaestiones super librum de causis*, he should not have had difficulty with Stephen Tempier and his censors in 1277. If we may safely assume that they had access to this treatise, it is clear that, at least in this case, they were not moved by Siger's change of view. They were still undoubtedly aware of his pre-1270 views on unicity of the intellect and so, without naming him, once again condemned the position Bishop Tempier had previously condemned in 1270. Thus propositions 117-32, and 126-121 are directed against unicity of the (possible) intellect or against the denial that it is

the form of the body. For the latter also see propositions 120-105, 121-11, 125-119.[114]

Interestingly, in q. 12 of this same work Siger
examines the issue of the eternity of the created Intelligence. After presenting arguments for and against
this, he concludes that because the authority of the
Christian faith is greater than any human argumentation and greater than the authority of the philosophers, we should hold that the Intelligence does not
exist from eternity even though we have no demonstration to prove this. Moreover, in a move that brings
him closer to Aquinas's position both on the faith-
reason issue and on eternity of the world, he adds
that the arguments supporting eternity of the Intelligence are not necessary and then attempts to resolve them philosophically.[115]

On the other hand, Siger's discussion in q. 28
of another sensitive issue may have provoked some
uneasiness in the minds of Tempier and his advisers,
assuming again that they read it. Be that as it may,
in this question Siger asks whether the essence of
the First Cause can be understood by our intellect. Siger
offers a number of arguments in support of this claim,
and then another series of arguments against it. But he
does not decide the question either way, or even indicate why he leaves it undecided. Perhaps we have lost
his determination of this question.[116]

This particular issue was troubling to Tempier
and his advisers, so much so that they seem to have
been inconsistent on this matter and to have con-

demned both the view that we can arrive at some kind of knowledge of God's essence in this life, and that we cannot. Thus prohibited proposition 9-36 holds that we can know God through his essence. But condemned proposition 10-215 asserts that we can only know of God that he is, or that he exists. Godfrey of Fontaines was pleased to point out some years later the incompatibility of Tempier's condemning both of these propositions at the same time.[117]

As for Siger, in most of his discussions of our knowledge of God, he holds that we know him by reasoning from knowledge of his effects to knowledge of him as their cause. This, of course, is perfectly orthodox. But in one manuscript version (Munich) of his *Quaestiones in Metaphysicam,* at III, 1, he asks whether it is impossible for us to know the First Cause essentially. He comments that some hold that it is impossible for us to have essential knowledge of the First Cause and of separate substance, but that Averroes holds the opposite view. After some discussion he offers the curious suggestion that it seems that someone who is deeply versed in philosophy can move from knowledge of the effects of the First Being to an understanding of its essence. This text is both puzzling in light of the view Siger has expressed elsewhere, and rather obscure in itself. It may have been envisioned by Tempier's advisers in formulating condemned proposition 9-36.[118]

In the main, however, we may conclude that in his *Quaestiones super librum de causis,* his final work so far as we know, Siger was much more concerned about reconciling his positions with Christian orthodoxy. We have already seen this with respect to his views on unicity vs. multiplicity of the possible intellect, and on eternity of the First Intelligence. Moreover, as mentioned above, in this work he clearly rejects the Neoplatonic theory of necessary and eternal emanation. In q. 36 he presents a number of arguments for and against the possibility that one immaterial substance might produce another. He then argues that the act of creating, that is, of producing the being (*esse*) of something from no presupposed subject, is restricted to the First Cause both according to the Platonists and in truth. Nor can the power to communicate *esse* without using any presupposed subject be communicated to an intelligence even as an instrument of the First Cause. Siger's reasoning here follows very closely that developed by Aquinas in, for instance, his *De potentia*, his *Summa contra gentiles*, and his *Summa theologiae*.[119]

While our knowledge of Siger's final years is very sketchy indeed, it is clear that he, along with two other Masters in Arts, Bernier of Nivelles and Gosvin de la Chapelle, were cited in a document issued on November 23, 1276, to appear before the French Inquisitor in January 1277, and hence well before the Condemnation of March 7, 1277. It seems likely that he and the others had already departed from the kingdom of France and that Siger himself went to Italy, where, it has been suggested, he was placed under some kind of house arrest but provided with a secretary. There is no indication that he was ever found guilty of the crime of heresy. Some time before November 10, 1284, he died, having been slain, perhaps by his secretary. But he would be immortalized by Dante in the *Divine Comedy*, who places him in Paradise and has St. Thomas Aquinas introduce him. It has been suggested that Dante may have been aware of Siger's moves in a more orthodox direction in his final work.[120]

Before leaving Siger's views on faith and reason, it will be helpful for us to turn to his only explicit discussion of the relationship between philosophy and theology as this is preserved in two of the surviving manuscript versions of his *Quaestiones in Metaphysicam*. As Armand Maurer has shown in a recent study, Siger's discussion here follows very closely Thomas Aquinas's presentation of *sacra doctrina* in q. 1 of *Summa theologiae* I.[121]

As does Thomas in his discussion in the *Summa* and elsewhere, Siger recognizes two kinds of theology—sacred theology or what Siger himself calls the science of theology that is Sacred Scripture, and another theology which is a part of philosophy. He begins by referring to Aristotle's *Metaphysics* VI, 1 (1026a18-19) where the Stagirite notes that there are three theoretical sciences—natural philosophy, mathematics, and theology. Siger comments that the science of being as being deserves to be called theology, as is evident from Aristotle's text. Since both

this science and Sacred Scripture are known as theology, he proposes to show how they differ. In close
correspondence with Thomas's discussion in the
Summa, Siger brings out six differences between the
two kinds of theology.[122]

First, they differ as regards their respective ways
of proceeding. The theology that is a part of philosophy proceeds from principles which are known
by the light of natural or human reason and discovered from sense perception, memory, and experience
(see *Posterior Analytics* II, 19). The theology Siger
refers to as Sacred Scripture proceeds not from such
naturally knowable principles but from principles
made known to us through divine revelation. According to the Vienna manuscript, this theology proceeds from such revealed principles through human
inquiry, by applying these principles to other things
so as to draw conclusions. This is an important observation since it means that for Siger this theology in-
volves much more than a simple inspection of the contents of Scripture and, indeed, sounds very much like
Aquinas's understanding of sacred theology (*sacra
doctrina, theologia*), the theology based on Scripture.[123]

Second, the two theologies differ with respect
to the things considered in each. The philosopher's
theology treats of God only in terms of what can be
discovered about him by human reason as it moves
from knowledge of effects to knowledge of him as
their cause. The theology Siger calls Sacred Scripture considers such things as well as others that are

beyond human reason's ability to discover. Hence whatever things are contained in revelation, whether they are natural beings, divine beings, or mathematicals, or even Siger adds, something else, so long as they are or can be known through revelation, will fall under this theology.[124]

Third, as following from the second difference, Siger notes that the philosopher's theology is less universal than is the other. This is because it is limited to what can be grasped by human reason, while the other theology considers both such things and others which are above human reason. Moreover, if the theology that is a part of philosophy, i.e., metaphysics, can concern itself with the principles of the particular sciences, it should not involve itself with the conclusions drawn by such sciences. The theology named Sacred Scripture can concern itself with both the principles and the conclusions of all the sciences to the extent that they are contained in revelation.[125]

Fourth, (according to the order of the Cambridge text and of Thomas's discussion in the *Summa*), Siger notes that the theology he calls Sacred Scripture is more practical than is the philosopher's theology (metaphysics). Two reasons support this, he adds. The first type of theology can deal with all things which can be known through revelation, and these can be either theoretical or practical. The theology of the philosopher (metaphysics) is a theoretical science only. Moreover, revelation is really nothing else but a certain imprint (*impressio*) of the divine science (cf. Thomas, ST I, q. 1, a. 3, ad 2). But in God there is no distinction between theoretical and practical science.[126]

Fifth, they differ because the theology known as Sacred Scripture is more certain than is the theology which is a part of philosophy. This is so because certitude in a science follows from the certitude it has with respect to its principles. The principles from which the theology referred to as Sacred Scripture proceeds are better known and more certain than are those from which the philosopher's theology proceeds. This is so because the principles of the first-mentioned theology are given to us through revelation, and error cannot enter into such knowledge, maintains Siger. The principles from which the philosopher's theology proceeds are known by way of sense perception, memory, and experience, and error can enter into our grasp of these principles. This admission on Siger's part about the possibility of philosophy's being in error in its grasp of its own principles is important; for it suggests some justification in Siger's mind for holding that something might be demonstrated necessarily as following from philosophical principles and yet not be true, as Aquinas believed Siger maintained.[127]

Sixth, the two theologies differ because the one called Sacred Scripture is wisdom to a greater degree than is the one which is a part of philosophy. In the Vienna manuscript Siger here refers back to Aristotle's well known discussion of wisdom in *Meta-*

physics I, c. 2 and recalls that that science is called wisdom which deals with first causes and principles, that is, with God and other separate substances. Siger concludes from this that the science which has greater and more certain knowledge of the first principles of beings is more entitled to be called wisdom. This, he maintains, is truer of the theology he calls Sacred Scripture than of the philosopher's theology.[128]

In summing this up, Siger states that, as things now appear to him, these two theologies differ in the six ways he has enumerated. He adds that those proceed in the worst way who would use the path of demonstration in all matters dealt with in the theology he refers to as Sacred Scripture.[129]

In this text, assuming again, as I am ready to do, that we can take it at face value, Siger is very far from being a rationalist. Here he is certainly willing to give its due to the theology based on revelation, and hence to revelation itself. At the same time, very significant from the standpoint of philosophical evaluation is Siger's acknowledgment that error may enter into the metaphysician's grasp of the first principles of metaphysics or of philosophical theology. As we have noted, this admission suggests that Siger may indeed have been sincere in other passages where he has pointed to a difference between what the philosophers or philosophy teach, and what the faith teaches, and concludes that in such cases one must follow the teaching of faith.[130]

At the same time, his statement points to a rather unhappy balance, an unresolved tension, between faith and reason and between theology and philosophy. On this point his position differs greatly from that of Aquinas, who would never have admitted that something could be necessarily demonstrated in a philosophical science and yet not be true. Siger is clearly not defending a double truth theory, since he does not maintain that a philosophical position which contradicts the teaching of faith is itself true. But in his effort to give sufficient weight to the teaching of faith and to the theology he refers to as Sacred Scripture, he now seems to have fallen into the opposite extreme. He has cast some doubt upon the certainty the philosopher or the metaphysician can have in grasping the first principles of metaphysics. While he gives the appearance of one who is struggling to harmonize faith and reason, he does not seem to have ever managed to do so in such a way that does full justice to the claims of both.[131]

Before leaving Siger's discussion of the two kinds of theology, reference should be made to one contested point. With A. Maurer we have assumed when comparing Siger's treatment with that of Aquinas in his *Summa theologiae* that by the theology Siger refers to as Sacred Scripture he really has in mind essentially the same thing as Thomas's understanding of sacred theology or *sacra doctrina*. Maurer has been challenged on this point in two articles by T. B. Bukowski.[132] In addition to the secondary sources

already cited by Maurer in support of his reading
(Chenu, Congar, Gilby, to whom one may add E.
Persson), additional evidence may be drawn from
another and much earlier work, Thomas's Commentary on the *De Trinitate*. There in q. 2, a. 2 he distinguishes two "divine sciences," one pursued by the
philosophers who referred to their first philosophy
by this title, and another in which those truths we
hold on faith serve as principles from which we de-
rive conclusions. This observation closely resembles
a point made by Siger in discussing the first difference between the two theologies.[133]

In q. 5, a. 4 of this same Commentary Thomas
works out in detail the distinction between the two
theologies or divine sciences. In one we consider divine things not as the subject of the science, but as
principles of the subject of this science, i.e., of being
as being. This, writes Thomas, is the theology pursued by the philosophers, which is also known as
metaphysics. In the other one considers divine things
for their own sake as the subject of the science. This is
the theology which is "handed down in Sacred Scripture," and which Thomas also here refers to as the "theology of Sacred Scripture." Such usage could easily lead
Siger to refer to this theology as Sacred Scripture.[134]

Finally, in an extremely interesting discussion in Albert
the Great's *Summa* (Tr. I, qq. 1-5), the German Dominican repeatedly moves back and forth between the terms
sacra scriptura and theology. Hence, against Bukowski's
challenge, it seems clear enough that one is quite justified

in taking Siger's theology, which he calls Sacred Scripture, as fundamentally the same as Aquinas's understanding of sacred theology.[135] There were enough historical precedents for Siger to adopt such terminology.

3: *Boethius of Dacia.*

As we have already indicated, the other primary target of Tempier's Condemnation in 1277 was Boethius of Dacia. Little is known about his life and career, but he clearly played an important role as a Master of Arts at Paris in the early 1270s. While a number of the propositions condemned by Tempier were taken from his writings, his name is not included among the three cited in November 1276 to appear before the French Inquisition. At the same time, almost nothing is known with certainty about his career after the Condemnation of 1277. An early fourteenth-century bibliographical catalog for the Dominican order, the Catalog of Stams, suggests that he may have eventually become a Dominican.[136] We are now fortunate to have good critical editions of almost all his known surviving works. Two of these are of special interest with respect to his views on the faith-reason issue, i.e., his treatise *On the Supreme Good* and his treatise *On the Eternity of the World.*

His treatise *On the Supreme Good* has been interpreted differently by various modern scholars. In this work Boethius indicates that his purpose here is to determine by reason the supreme good available to human beings. From the beginning he makes it clear that he is here offering a philosophical analysis of this issue. After distinguishing between the speculative intellect and the practical intellect, he argues that the supreme good available to human beings by reason of the speculative intellect is knowledge of what is true and delight in the same. Such knowledge includes awareness of all things which are caused by the First Being, and, in so far as such is possible for us, knowledge of and delight in the First Being itself. The supreme good available to us by reason of our practical intellect is right action, i.e., to do what is good and to take delight in it. Boethius reasons that by combining the good of the speculative intellect and that of the practical intellect we may conclude that the supreme good available to us is to know what is true, to do what is good, and to delight in both.[137]

And then he observes that because the supreme good which is possible for a human being is happiness (*beatitudo*), it follows that human happiness consists in knowing what is true, doing what is good, and taking delight in both. In his only reference to religious belief and to life after death in this entire treatise, he notes that one who does attain more perfectly that happiness which reason tells us is possible in this life approaches more closely that "happiness which we expect in the life to come on the authority of faith."[138]

Farther on in this treatise Boethius comments on the small number of human beings who really successfully pursue this supreme good. These indi-

viduals should be held in high honor, he argues, because they alone pursue the pleasure of reason and reject pleasures of the senses and thereby live according
to the natural order. Such men, he adds, are the philosophers. Boethius extols the life of the philosopher,
and especially insofar as such a person arrives at knowledge of God, the First Cause. Boethius condemns anyone who does not lead such a life: "Whoever does not
live such a life does not live rightly." He does concede
that by the philosopher he has in mind anyone who
lives in accord with nature and who has attained the
ultimate end of human life—God himself.[139]

Some modern interpreters have concluded that
Boethius defends an unqualified rationalism in this treatise, or at least that he strongly tends to that extreme.
Others emphasize the point that this is intended to be
a purely philosophical discussion and they find nothing in it contrary to Christian faith. Boethius has indicated that in this work he wants to determine the highest good available to human beings by using reason
alone, without relying on religious belief.[140]

I myself find this consistent with Boethius's insistence in his *De aeternitate mundi* on one's obliga-
tion to pursue any given human field of learning in
accord with the principles and methodology of that
discipline. Even so, it must also be acknowledged
that the *De summo bono* could easily be read by Christian thinkers of Boethius's day or, for that matter, of
our own, as trumpeting a kind of philosophical imperialism. Examination of his *De aeternitate mundi*

suggests that Boethius at least intended to avoid con-
flict between faith and reason. Nonetheless, the *De
summo bono* may well have been targeted by
Tempier's condemnation of proposition 1-40: "There
is no more excellent kind of life than to give oneself
to philosophy." Theologians, churchmen, and religious mystics would not have been pleased with this.

But Boethius himself could reply that in his treatise *On the Supreme Good* he is led to this conclusion
by depending on philosophical principles and on
reason alone, not by taking into account revealed
data. The treatise is also noteworthy in that it illus-
trates how by ca. 1270 a Master of Arts could strongly
argue for the value of pursuing a career in Arts, i.e.,
in philosophy rather than merely as a stepping-stone
to a career in a higher faculty, e.g., Theology. This
attitude was sharply condemned by Henry of Ghent,
along with any suggestion that speculative philosophy might be pursued for its own sake.[141]

In his *On the Eternity of the World* Boethius begins
by recognizing the distinction between faith and reason, i.e., between that which can be accepted only on
the strength of the Law (revelation) and other things
which are amenable to rational or philosophical argumentation. He cautions against any attempt to demonstrate philosophically that which can be held solely
on faith. And he states that in writing this treatise he
intends to bring into harmony the view of Christian
faith concerning the eternity of the world, and the
position held by Aristotle and other philosophers.[142]

Boethius offers three reasons for making this effort: (1) to protect the position taught by faith; (2) to defend the position of the philosophers to the extent conclusive rational argumentation can be offered for it; and (3) to show that faith and philosophy do not contradict one another on this topic.[143]

After offering a long series of arguments against an eternal world, he presents two sets of arguments for the opposed position. The first set attempts to show that an eternal world is possible, and the second set argues that the world is indeed eternal.[144] In developing his own solution, Boethius asserts the philosopher's right to discuss any question which can be disputed by rational argumentation. Even though this text and another which parallels it could be given a perfectly orthodox interpretation, it was probably the target of another proposition on Tempier's list. Condemned proposition 6-145 reads: "That there is no question which can be disputed by reason which the philosopher should not dispute and determine, because rational arguments are derived from things. But it belongs to philosophy in its various parts to consider all things."[145]

Indeed, inspired by Aristotle's discussion in *Metaphysics* IV and by his threefold division of theoretical philosophy in Bk VI of the *Metaphysics*, Boethius notes that if philosophy studies being, the various parts of philosophy examine the various parts or kinds of being. Since the philosopher investigates all parts of being, natural, mathematical, and divine, he is entitled to determine any question which can be disputed rationally. But of the three kinds of theoretical philosopher, i.e., the natural philosopher, the mathematician, and the metaphysician, none can prove that the world (and the first motion) began to be.[146] So long as one remembers that Boethius is speaking here as a philosopher, and defending the philosopher's right to examine all that can be investigated in the light of reason, one should not regard his view as worthy of condemnation. Nonetheless, his remarks could again be taken as suggesting a kind of philosophical imperialism which would be offensive to the theologians.

As for the particular point at issue, eternity of the world, most interesting for our purposes is Boethius's effort to show that the natural philosopher cannot prove that the world began to be. One who practices a given science can demonstrate, grant or deny something only in terms of the principles of that science. Moreover, although nature is not the First Principle in the absolute sense, it is the first principle for natural things and hence the first principle that the natural philosopher can consider[147].

So far as the natural philosopher can determine, no new motion can be caused except by another motion which is prior to it in time. Hence, the first motion cannot have begun to be, for then it would not be first but would be preceded by still another prior motion. Therefore, the natural philosopher, by reasoning in accord with the principles of natural philosophy, cannot hold that the first motion ever began to be or that the world began to be.[148]

Boethius also concludes from this that the natural philosopher cannot even examine the issue of creation, i.e., the production of something from no preexisting subject, since nature produces its effects only from a (preexisting) subject and from matter. Nor can the natural philosopher, *qua* natural philosopher, ever show that there was a first human being since the first human could not be generated.[149]

Still Boethius is well aware that it is true according to Christian faith and, he adds, true in the absolute sense that the world did begin to be, that creation is possible, that there was a first human being, and that the dead will return as numerically one and the same as their former selves at the resurrection. Hence one may counter that the natural philosopher should not deny any of these truths, even if he cannot demonstrate them.[150]

In response to this objection Boethius reasons that the natural philosopher should not deny truths which do not follow from the principles of natural philosophy if these truths are not contrary to the principles of that science and do not destroy it. But the natural philosopher should deny any truth which cannot be known or proved from the principles of natural philosophy if that truth is opposed to its principles and destroys it itself. Therefore the natural philosopher, always speaking as a natural philosopher, should deny that a dead person can return immediately to life, or that a thing subject to generation can be brought into being without being generated. Yet because of belief in the resurrection, the Christian rightly holds that the dead will return as numerically one and the same as their former selves. The natural philosopher will deny such truths because as a natural philosopher, he should grant nothing which is not possible through purely natural causes. Even so, adds Boethius, the Christian rightly accepts these things as possible on the strength of revelation, because they are produced by a higher cause which is the cause of all nature. Therefore the Christian and the natural philosopher do not contradict one another on these matters or on other points.[151]

Boethius goes on to show that neither the mathematician nor the metaphysician can prove that the world began to be, and therefore, that no philosopher can do so. In defending this position he is in agreement with Siger of Brabant, to be sure, but at least as regards this conclusion, he is also in agreement with Thomas Aquinas. But he is opposed to Bonaventure as he is commonly interpreted, and, as his subsequent writings would show, to Henry of Ghent, to name but two of the more conservative theologians.[152]

Boethius goes on to deny that philosophical argumentation can prove that the world is eternal and refutes each of the arguments he had offered in support of this. On this point he is also in agreement with Aquinas as well as with the more conservative group of theologians. He agrees with them that faith teaches us many things which human reason cannot demonstrate.[153]

One point must be made clear here. Boethius is not defending the infamous double-truth theory to which Bishop Tempier referred in the introduction to his Condemnation of 1277, even though he has been suspected of this by some. He is not claiming that philosophical argumentation can demonstrate that the position asserting eternity of the world is true in the absolute sense. Speaking as a Christian, he maintains that only the position made known to us through revelation—that the world began to be— is true in the absolute sense. But his way of making his point could easily be misinterpreted. For he has also written that one can say, speaking as a Christian, that the world began to be, and yet that the natural philosopher speaks the truth in denying that the world and first motion began to be.[154]

If Boethius had said no more, one might accuse him of defending a double-truth theory. But he immediately adds that this is so because the natural philosopher denies, *as* a natural philosopher, that the world began to be. By this the natural philosopher means that the world and the first motion did not begin to be from natural causes and principles. Whatever the natural philosopher *as* a natural philosopher denies or grants, he does so from natural causes and principles. If the Christian speaks the absolute truth by professing that the world did begin to be, the natural philosopher also speaks the truth by denying that such things are possible from natural causes and principles. Hence Boethius also writes confidently that "the natural philosopher does not contradict Christian faith concerning eternity of the world."[155]

Even so, Boethius's way of expressing this point is somewhat provocative. Provocative also is a remark which he makes near the end of his treatise and which appears to be directed against Bishop Tempier: "If, however, someone, whether enjoying a position of dignity or not, cannot understand such difficult matters, then let him obey the wise man and let him believe in the Christian Law." Boethius strongly warns against attempting to justify faith by relying on sophistical argumentation (which deceives) or dialectical reasoning (which can only justify probable assent) or even on demonstrative argumentation. He comments that demonstration is not possible with respect to all the things our Law, i.e., our religious faith, holds and, in addition, that demonstration produces science, whereas faith is not science.[156]

CONCLUSION

Boethius's protests of loyalty to the faith did him little good, for in addition to those already mentioned, a number of other propositions contained in Tempier's list of 1277 were apparently taken from his writings.[157] But of greater interest to our immediate topic is another issue. While defending an ultimate harmony between reason and revelation, Boethius has proposed a solution which upholds the fundamental autonomy and the intrinsic integrity of philosophy, and this was of great importance to him.

Curiously, however, his solution also seems to run the risk of putting in doubt the certainty of at least some properly demonstrated philosophical conclusions. Thus he has acknowledged that the natural philosopher, by proceeding correctly as a purely natural philosopher, may reach conclusions which necessarily follow from the principles of natural philosophy, and which, while they are truly and correctly derived from those principles, are not true in the absolute sense. Here one is reminded of Siger of Brabant's admission of the possibility that the philosopher may be in error even in grasping some philosophical principles, and presumably, therefore, in deriving conclusions therefrom. Such solutions to the faith-reason problem seem to undercut the degree of certainty a Thomas Aquinas would assign both to the first principles of natural philosophy and the other parts of speculative philosophy, and to any conclusions which are correctly derived from them.

According to Siger, some philosophical principles, and according to Boethius, some conclusions which necessarily follow from philosophical principles, might nonetheless be false. Yet we would not know this except for the additional information given to us by divine revelation. These approaches seem to cast philosophical conclusions (for Boethius) and even philosophical principles (for Siger) in a somewhat hypothetical light. They will be regarded as true by the philosopher unless the Christian revelation tells us that they are not!

Both Siger, at least the mature Siger, and Boethius of Dacia were concerned with harmonizing faith and reason, as was Thomas Aquinas. For Aquinas, however, the approach advanced by the two Masters in Arts would not have been fully satisfactory. It would, in his eyes, compromise some of the confidence one can place in the power of human reason to arrive at truth in purely philosophical issues, if and when those issues touch on matters also dealt with by revelation. Curiously enough, their efforts to reconcile faith and reason, and at the same time, to protect the intrinsic integrity and autonomy of purely philosophical inquiry, end by paying a considerable price, i.e., by placing the certainty of purely philosophical inquiry at risk or in question when dealing with certain issues. Because of Thomas's insistence that both reason and revelation stem from one and the same source, God himself, and because God cannot contradict himself, Thomas maintains that reason when rightly exercised cannot contradict revelation when that is rightly interpreted. On this point at least, it seems to me that Thomas has spoken better than have Boethius and Siger.

Aquinas's distinctive philosophical and theological positions did not win unanimous acceptance either within his lifetime or during the fifty years or so between his death and his canonization. Whether or not one holds that he was directly targeted by the Condemnation of 1277, it is generally agreed that he was at least indirectly implicated. As we have seen, a number of positions which he had defended were included in the list of prohibited propositions. If Wielockx is correct in thinking that a separate process had already been set in motion against Aquinas himself by Tempier in March 1277, this simply strengthens our point. Moreover, his theory of unicity of substantial form in human beings was condemned by the Archbishop of Canterbury, Robert Kilwardby, in 1277, and again in 1284 and 1286 by his successor, Archbishop John Pecham.[158]

Not long after his death a controversial work listing alleged errors taught by Aquinas was written by the Franciscan William de la Mare, and this in turn generated a series of replies by Dominican defenders of Aquinas.[159] Among secular Masters at Paris in the decades following his death, the two most outstanding were Henry of Ghent and Godfrey of Fontaines. Henry's opposition to Aquinas on various philosophical and theological points is well known and has been mentioned above. He defended the priority of faith over reason and of theology over purely human disciplines including philosophy in a way that is reminiscent of Augustine and Bonaventure.[160]

Godfrey was much more sympathetic to Aquinas and his version of Aristotelianism, but also differed with him on a number of important philosophical issues including one regarded by most

Thomistic scholars as absolutely central to his metaphysics, the theory of real distinction or real com-
position of essence and *esse* in created entities.[161]

Even so, on the faith-reason issue Godfrey's practice reveals that here he was in fundamental agreement with Aquinas. And concerning this issue, the
judgement of history has ultimately supported Aquinas. His solution to the faith-reason problem is still,
in my opinion, the most satisfactory one developed
by any medieval Christian thinker.

NOTES

1. For the text of this condemnation see H. Denifle and A. Chatelain, *Chartularium Universitatis Parisiensis* I (Paris, 1889), pp. 543-58; also listed in a systematic reordering in P. Mandonnet, *Siger de Brabant et l'Averroïsme latin au XIIIe siècle*, 2nd ed., 2 vols. (Louvain, 1911, 1908), Vol II, pp. 175-91. When citing propositions from this condemnation, I will first give the Mandonnet number and then the *Chartularium* number.

2. Mandonnet ed., p. 175. Note especially: "... quasi sint duae contrariae veritates, et quasi contra veritatem sacrae Scripturae sit veritas in dictis gentilium damnatorum...."

3. For a good overview of this issue in English see F. Van Steenberghen, *Thomas Aquinas and Radical Aristotelianism* (Washington, D.C., 1980), pp. 93-109. For Boethius of Dacia's highly nuanced and sometimes misinterpreted position on this see Part III, 3 below.

4. See *De libero arbitrio*, Bk II, cc. ii-xv. Note especially Augustine's comment in c. xv: "Est enim deus et vere summeque est. Quod iam non solum indubitatum, quantum arbitror, fide retinemus, sed etiam certa, quamvis adhuc tenuissima forma cognitionis adtingimus...." (c. xv, CCSL vol. 29, p. 264).

5. See c. ii, p. 239: "Nisi enim et aliud esset credere, aliud intellegere et primo credendum esset quod magnum et divinum intellegere cuperemus, frustra propheta dixisset: *Nisi credideritis, non intellegetis.*"

6. For an excellent general introduction to Boethius see H. Chadwick, *Boethius. The Consolations of Music, Logic, Theology, and Philosophy* (Oxford, 1981). On his *De Hebdomadibus* see pp. 203-11. Also see G. Schrimpf, *Die Axiomenschrift des Boethius (De*

Hebdomadibus) als philosophisches Lehrbuch des Mittelalters (Leiden, 1966). On Boethius's *Consolation of Philosophy* see, in addition to Chadwick (pp. 223-47), P. Courcelle, *La consolation de philosophie dans la tradition littéraire: antécédents et postérité de Boèce* (Paris, 1967). Also of importance on Boethius is L. Obertello, *Severino Boezio*, 2 vols (Genoa, 1974). In his *Scholasticism: Personalities and Problems of Medieval Philosophy* (New York-Toronto, 1964), J. Pieper gives Boethius high praise for his explicit call to join faith and reason (see p. 37).

7. The first two surviving Boethian translations of Aristotle's logical works, the *Categories* and the *De interpretatione*, along with Porphyry's *Isagoge* came to be known as the Old Logic (*Logica vetus*). The later recovered translations or new translation (in the case of the *Posterior Analytics*) in the high middle ages came to be known as the New Logic (*Logica nova*). For an overview see B. Dod, "Aristoteles Latinus," in *The Cambridge History of Later Medieval Philosophy*, N. Kretzmann, A. Kenny, J. Pinborg, eds. (Cambridge, 1982), pp. 46ff.

8. For a valuable study of this work see I. Resnick, *Divine Power and Possibility in St. Peter Damian's De Divina Omnipotentia* (Leiden, New York, Köln, 1992). For the text see the edition by A. Cantin, *Lettre sur la toute-puissance divine* (Sources Chrétiennes, Paris, 1972).

9. See *Anselm of Canterbury. Truth, Freedom, and Evil: Three Philosophical Dialogues*, J. Hopkins and H. Richardson, eds. and trs. (Harper Torchbooks, 1967), p. 10. Hopkins comments that the *De Grammatico* is an exception "because it serves purely as a philosophical manual providing training in dialectic and having no ostensible connection with theology." See his *A*

Companion to the Study of St. Anselm (Minneapolis, 1972), p. 5. For text, translation and study see D. Henry, *The De Grammatico of St. Anselm: The Theory of Paronymy* (Notre Dame, Ind., 1964).

10. For the Latin text, English translation, and helpful introductions see J. Hopkins, *A New, Interpretive Translation of St. Anselm's Monologion and Proslogion* (Minneapolis, 1986); M. J. Charlesworth, *St. Anselm's Proslogion* (Oxford, 1965). It will be evident to the reader that I do not accept the fideistic readings of the *Proslogion* proposed earlier in this century by K. Barth and A. Stolz, as does neither Charlesworth nor Hopkins. See Charlesworth, pp. 40-46, and Hopkins, *A Companion*, pp. 38-43, 56-63.

11. See *S. Anselmi Cantuariensis Archiepiscopi opera omnia*, F. S. Schmitt, ed., Vol. 2 (repr. Stuttgart-Bad Cannstatt, 1968 in T. 1), p. 42 (Preface): "Ac tandem remoto Christo, quasi numquam aliquid fuerit de illo, probat rationibus necessariis esse impossibile ullum hominem salvari sine illo." Also see his reference in the same context (pp. 42-43) to his intention in writing the second book. There he intends to show by relying on reason that human nature was created in order that the entire human being, including body and soul, should enjoy blessed immortality, and that this in turn could only be achieved through the man-God, and hence that it was necessary for all that we believe concerning Christ to come to pass.

12. *Ed. cit.*, p. 47.

13. That Anselm intends to prove God's existence in the *Proslogion* is indicated not only by the Preface and by the end of ch. 4, but is reinforced by his Reply to Gaunilo. In the latter see his summary in section X.

For Anselm's concern with meeting objections raised
by unbelievers (*infideles*) against the Incarnation see
Cur Deus Homo, Bk I, c. 1, *ed. cit.*, pp. 47-48. Also see
Proslogion, Prooemium, where Anselm notes that he
had first called his *Monologion* an "Exemplum
meditandi de ratione fidei" and the *Proslogion* "Fides
quaerens intellectum" (see Schmitt ed., Vol. 1, p. 94).

14. For an overview of the newly translated philosophical
literature see Dod, "Aristoteles Latinus," c. 2, in *The
Cambridge History of Later Medieval Philosophy*, pp. 45-
79; F. Van Steenberghen, *La philosophie au XIIIe siècle*,
2nd ed. (Louvain-Paris, 1991), pp. 67-107.

15. See Dod, p. 46, for the points that the remaining
Boethian translations of Aristotle's logical writings,
i.e., the *Prior Analytics, Topics*, and *Sophistici elenchi*,
were recovered "from about 1120 onwards," and that
these were completed by James of Venice's translation
from the Greek of the *Posterior Analytics* between
?1125 and 1150 (also see p. 75). Although some of
these became available in Latin during Abelard's lifetime and although he cites at least one of them, the *Prior
Analytics*, J. Marenbon points out that "it is a text which
neither he nor his contemporaries had absorbed into the
mainstream of their logical thought." See *Early Medieval
Philosophy (480-1150)* (London, 1983), p. 131.

16. See *Petrus Abaelardus. Dialogus inter Philosophum,
Judaeum et Christianum* (Stuttgart-Bad Cannstatt,
1970), and English translation by P. J. Payer, *Peter
Abelard. A Dialogue of a Philosopher with a Jew, and a
Christian* (Toronto, 1979). Also see *Peter Abelard's
Ethics*, by D. E. Luscombe (Oxford, 1971), for text
and English translation. Note his remarks on Abelard's
Dialogus, pp. xxv-xxx.

17. For a sympathetic portrayal of Abelard's views on this see R. E. Weingart, *The Logic of Divine Love. A Critical Analysis of the Soteriology of Peter Abelard* (Oxford, 1970), c. 1 ("*Theologia*: the Dialectic of Faith and Reason").

18. See n. 14 above. For fuller bibliography on the translations from Arabic into Latin see H. Daiber, "Lateinische Übersetzungen arabischer Texte zur Philosophie und ihre Bedeutung für die Scholastik des Mittelalter. Stand und Aufgabe der Forschung," in *Rencontres de cultures dans la philosophie médiévale. Traductions et traducteurs de l'Antiquité tardive au XIVe siècle.* J. Hamesse and M. Fattori, eds. (Louvain-la-Neuve-Cassino, 1990), pp. 203-50.

19. For the texts of the synod of 1210 and of the Statutes of 1215 prohibiting lecturing on these works see *Chartularium...*, I, p. 70, n. 11; pp. 78-79, n. 20. On this see M. Grabmann, *I divieti ecclesiastici di Aristotele sotto Innocenzo III e Gregorio IX* (Rome, 1941), c. 1, and Van Steenberghen, *La philosophie au XIIIe siècle*, pp. 82-89.

20. For the letter of July 7, 1228, see *Chartularium*, I, pp. 114-16, n. 59; for the pertinent letter of April 13, 1231, see *Chartularium*, I, p. 138, n. 79. For the letter establishing and charging the commission with their task, see *Chartularium*, I, pp. 143-44. On all of this see Grabmann, *I divieti*, c. 2, pp. 70-108; Van Steenberghen, *La philosophie au XIIIe siècle*, pp. 98-101.

21. On work by Masters in Arts until 1240, see Van Steenberghen, *La philosophie*, pp. 109-30. On Bacon's role, see pp. 130-37. On the Neoplatonic elements in the Aristotelianism of the Masters in Theology between 1225-1250, see pp. 157, 169-76. For the Statutes of 1255 for the Faculty of Arts, see *Chartularium*, I, pp. 277-279, n. 246.

22. On Albert the Great's role see Van Steenberghen, *La philosophie*, pp. 245-75 (including his review of his dialogue with B. Nardi on the proper appreciation of Albert's contributions and Albert's intention in writing his Aristotelian commentaries). Were they intended to be straightforward presentations of Aristotle's positions (Nardi) or did Albert also use them to reflect his personal philosophical positions (Van Steenberghen)? For a strong effort to reevaluate Albert's philosophical contributions without measuring him against or subordinating him to Aquinas see A. de Libera, *Albert le Grand et la philosophie* (Paris, 1990). While very useful as a corrective of misrepresentations of Albert's role in the development of thirteenth-century philosophy and of radical Aristotelianism, de Libera's book may need some correction, at least in its claim that Albert is the founder of "Latin Averroism." See pp. 21-22, 38, 268-69. Cf. Van Steenberghen's review in *Revue philosophique de Louvain* 89 (1991), pp. 312-13. For a very balanced assessment of Albert's influence on "Latin Averroism," see A. Zimmermann, "Albertus Magnus und der lateinische Averroismus," in *Albertus Magnus. Doctor Universalis 1280/1980*, G. Meyer and A. Zimmermann, eds. (Mainz, 1980), pp. 465-92.

23. One has a similar problem in interpreting Aquinas's Commentaries on Aristotle (see preceding note). Are they mere exercises in the history of philosophy, or expressions of his personal positions, or some combination of the two? For one concrete illustration and discussion of this from his Commentary on the *Metaphysics*, see my *Metaphysical Themes in Thomas Aquinas* (Washington, D.C., 1984), pp. 82-102.

24. Curiously, it seems to have taken some time for Christian readers of Averroes to discern in his Long Commentary on the *De anima* the theory of unicity of the possible intellect. Thus Roger Bacon when commenting on Aristotle's *libri naturales* believes that Averroes defends multiplicity of agent and possible intellects, as Albert the Great also believed in his *Summa de creaturis* (early 1240s). See Van Steenberghen, *La philosophie*, pp. 136, 252. Albert clearly did recognize and combat unicity of the (possible) intellect in his *De unitate intellectus contra Averroem*, presented orally at the Papal Court of Alexander IV in 1256 (Van Steenberghen, pp. 251ff.).

25. For a brief presentation of background concerning this, see my "The Condemnations of 1270 and 1277 at Paris," *The Journal of Medieval and Renaissance Studies* 7 (1977), pp. 169-201. More recent studies of the Condemnation of 1277 will be cited below.

26. For overviews concerning this, see Van Steenberghen, *Thomas Aquinas and Radical Aristotelianism* (Washington, D.C., 1980); *La philosophie...*, c. 8 ("L'aristotélisme hétérodoxe"), pp. 321-70.

27. For Bonaventure's Conferences of 1267, entitled *Collationes de decem praeceptis*, see *Opera omnia* (Quaracchi, 1882-1902), V, pp. 507-32. In Conference II he denounces as errors which follow from an improper employment of philosophical investigation eternity of the world, unicity of the intellect, and the denial that something mortal can arrive at immortality (pp. 514-15). For his Lenten Conferences of 1268 (*Collationes de septem donis Spiritus Sancti*), see *Opera omnia* V, pp. 457-98. In Conference IV he warns Christians against overevaluating philosophical science (pp. 474-76), and

in Conference VIII singles out a number of philosophical errors, for instance, that one intelligence can create another, and then three reprehensible errors, i.e., eternity of the world, the doctrine of fatal necessity, and unicity of the human intellect (p. 497).

28. See "Background to the Condemnation of 1270: Master William of Baglione, O.F.M.," *Franciscan Studies* 30 (1970), pp. 5-48. For Brady's related studies, see "Questions at Paris c. 1260-1270," *Archivum Franciscanum Historicum* 61 (1968), pp. 434-61; 62 (1969), pp. 357-76, 678-92; "The Questions of Master William of Baglione, O.F.M., *De aeternitate mundi* (Paris, 1266-1267)," *Antonianum* 47 (1972), pp. 362-71, 576-616. For a strong attack against the Averroistic theory of unicity of the intellect and its consequences, see "Background…," pp. 35-45. In dealing with the separated soul and the fire of hell, William explicitly refers to *philosophantes*, i.e., to Latin Christians engaged in philosophizing (p. 47).

29. *Chartularium*, I, pp. 486-87. For more on this, see Wippel, "The Condemnations…," pp. 179-82; Van Steenberghen, *Maître Siger de Brabant* (Louvain-Paris, 1977), pp. 74-79; *La philosophie…*, pp. 411-13.

30. For Siger's defense of unicity of the possible intellect in his *Quaestiones in Tertium de anima*, see q. 9 in *Quaestiones in Tertium de anima, De anima intellectiva, De aeternitate mundi*, B. Bazán, ed. (Louvain-Paris, 1972), pp. 25-29. Bazán proposes to date these questions in the 1269-1270 academic year, and more recently R.-A. Gauthier has proposed a date of ca. 1265. See his "Notes sur Siger de Brabant I," *Revue des Sciences philosophiques et théologiques* 67 (1983), p. 201. In this same study Gauthier has offered some

interesting textual corrections while also stressing the less than satisfactory character of the manuscript with which Bazán had to work (see pp. 206-08). In any event, this work clearly dates before the Condemnation of December 1270, and the *Quaestio utrum haec sit vera* most likely does. For its dating see *Siger de Brabant. Écrits de logique, de morale et de physique*, B. Bazán, ed. (Louvain-Paris, 1974), p. 25; Van Steenberghen, *Maître Siger* ..., pp. 50-51. Cf. L. Bianchi, *L'errore di Aristotele. La polemica contro l'eternità del mondo nel XIII secolo* (Florence, 1984), p. 87 and n. 48; "L'evoluzione dell'eternalismo di Sigeri di Brabante e la condanna del 1270," in *L'Homme et son Univers au Moyen Âge* (Actes du Septième Congrès International de Philosophie Médiévale), C. Wenin ed., Vol. 2 (Louvain-la-Neuve, 1986), pp. 904-05. For Siger's defense of eternity of the human species see *ed. cit.*, pp. 56-59. For his discussion of the separated soul and the fire of hell see his *Quaestiones in Tertium de Anima*, q. 11, pp. 31-35. Cf. Gauthier, pp. 217-26.

31. See *Chartularium*, I, pp. 486-87. The inability of the theory of unicity of the possible intellect to account for the testimony of consciousness indicating that each individual human being understands is a central part of Aquinas's philosophical refutation of this theory in his *De unitate intellectus* (see Part III below for this, and discussion in Van Steenberghen, *Maître Siger*, pp. 349, 354-55; *Thomas Aquinas and Radical Aristotelianism*, pp. 48, 56, 63-66). For an effort to defend Averroes from this part of Aquinas's rebuttal, see D. Black, "Consciousness and Self-Knowledge in Aquinas's Critique of Averroes's Psychology," *Journal of the History of Philosophy* 31 (1993), pp. 349-85. On

the continuity between Aquinas's general argumentation in this treatise and in earlier writings see E. P.
Mahoney, "Aquinas's Critique of Averroes' Doctrine
of the Unity of the Intellect," in *Thomas Aquinas and
his Legacy*, D. M. Gallagher, ed. (Washington, D.C.,
1994), pp. 83-106.

32. *Chartularium*, I, pp. 486-87.

33. For the text see *De unitate intellectus contra Averroistas*,
L. W. Keeler, ed. (Rome, 1957); Leonine ed., Vol. 43,
pp. 291-314. For an overview see Van Steenberghen,
Thomas Aquinas and Radical Aristotelianism, pp. 49-59.
On the title see p. 51, and Leonine ed., pp. 247b-248a.

34. Two *reportationes* of these conferences have survived
and been edited, the longer in Bonaventure's *Opera
omnia*, Vol. 5, and another edited by F. Delorme, *S.
Bonaventurae Collationes in Hexaëmeron et Bonaven-
turiana Quaedam Selecta* (Quaracchi, 1934).
Bonaventure's major attack occurs in Conference VI
(see Vol. 5, pp. 360-61 for longer version, and Delorme,
pp. 91-92). In Conference VI (longer version),
Bonaventure implies that these errors are still very
much alive, presumably at Paris, since he remarks that
some, recognizing that Aristotle was so outstanding in
other matters, cannot believe he was in error on these
issues (see p. 361). In Conference VII (longer version)
Bonaventure is somewhat more conciliatory in holding Aristotle responsible for three of the errors singled
out in Conference VI, i.e., eternity of the world,
unicity of the intellect, rejection of reward and punishment in the next life (p. 365). For discussion see
Van Steenberghen, *Maître Siger* ..., pp. 102-11.

35. See *Giles of Rome. Errores Philosophorum*, J. Koch, ed.
(Milwaukee, 1944), *passim*, and especially pp. 14-16

for unusually harsh words against Averroes. For dating see pp. lv-lix.

36. For Van Steenberghen's defense of this dating see his "Le 'De quindecim problematibus' d'Albert le Grand," repr. in his *Introduction à l'étude de la philosophie médiévale* (Louvain-Paris, 1974), pp. 433-55; *La philosophie au XIIIe siècle*, pp. 416-418, where he continues to defend a post-1270 date against the earlier dating proposed by Mandonnet, Geyer, Tresmontant, and Weisheipl (ca. Easter 1270). For Albert's response see his *De XV Problematibus*, B. Geyer, ed., *Opera omnia*, Vol. 17, Pt. 1 (Cologne, 1975). See p. xxi for Geyer's defense of the earlier date.

37. On this treatise see Van Steenberghen, *Maître Siger* ..., pp. 115-18. Reference to the anonymous commentaries will be made below.

38. For Pope John's letter see *Chartularium*, I, p. 541. While it is clear that Tempier had exceeded the mandate given him by the Pope in the latter's letter of January 18, we have no evidence that the Pope objected to Tempier's action. On the contrary, we do know that on April 28, 1277, the Pope addressed to Tempier a bull—*Flumen aquae vivae*—in which he ordered the Bishop to investigate errors being taught not only in Arts but also in Theology. See A. Callebaut, "Jean Pecham, O.F.M. et l'augustinisme. Aperçus historiques (1263-1285)," *Archivum Franciscanum Historicum* 18 (1925), pp. 458-61; A. Moreira de Sà, "Pedro Hispano e a crise de 1277 da Universidade de Paris," *Boletim da Biblioteca da Universidade de Coimbra* 22 (1954), pp. 221-41; E. Gilson, *History of Christian Philosophy in the Middle Ages* (New York, 1955), p. 727, n. 49; Van Steenberghen, *Maître Siger* ..., pp.

146-49. On Tempier see P. Glorieux, "Tempier, Etienne," *Dictionnaire de théologie catholique* 15 (1946), cols. 99-107. For Henry's membership on the commission see his *Quodlibet II*, q. 9, R. Wielockx, ed. (Leuven, 1983), p. 67:21-24.

39. See R. Hissette, *Enquête sur les 219 articles condamnés à Paris le 7 mars 1277* (Louvain-Paris, 1977); L. Bianchi, *Il Vescovo e i Filosofi. La condanna Parigina del 1277 e l'evoluzione dell'Aristotelismo scolastico* (Bergamo, 1990), with extensive bibliography (pp. 209-54); K. Flasch, *Aufklärung im Mittelalter? Die Verurteilung von 1277* (Mainz, 1989); Wippel, "The Condemnations of 1270 and 1277 at Paris," *Journal of Medieval and Renaissance Studies* 7 (1977), pp. 169-201 (published before Hissette's book); Hissette, "Etienne Tempier et les menaces contre l'éthique chrétienne," *Bulletin de philosophie médiévale* 21 (1979), pp. 68-72; "Etienne Tempier et ses condamnations," *Recherches de Théologie ancienne et médiévale* 47 (1980), pp. 231-70; "Note sur la réaction 'antimoderniste' d'Etienne Tempier," *Bulletin de Philosophie médiévale* 22 (1980), pp. 88-97.

40. See his *Quodlibet XII*, q. 5 (dating from 1296 or 1297) where he was asked to discuss this question: "Utrum Episcopus parisiensis peccet in hoc quod omittit corrigere quosdam articulos a praedecessore suo condemnatos" (*Les Philosophes Belges* V, pp. 100-04). For discussion see Wippel, *The Metaphysical Thought of Godfrey of Fontaines. A Study in Late Thirteenth-Century Philosophy* (Washington, D.C., 1981), pp. 382-85. On the dating of Godfrey's Quodlibets see pp. xxvii-xxviii.

41. For the text of this decree by Stephen of Bourret, then Bishop of Paris, see *Chartularium* II, pp. 280-81. On this see Bianchi, *Il Vescovo* ..., pp. 28-30, and notes; Hissette, "Albert le Grand et Thomas d'Aquin dans la censure Parisienne du 7 mars 1277," in *Miscellanea Mediaevalia* 15 (1982), pp. 231-32.

42. *In II Sententiarium*, d. 32, q. 2, a. 3 (Venice, 1581), p. 471. Note especially Giles's comment: "... plures de illis articulis transierunt non consilio Magistrorum sed capitositate quorumdam paucorum."

43. As noted above, we will give the Mandonnet numbering first, and then that found in the *Chartularium*.

44. Proposition 55-204: "Quod substantiae separatae sunt alicubi per operationem, et quod non possunt moveri ab extremo in extremum, nec in medium, nisi quia possunt velle operari aut in medio, aut in extremis.—Error, si intelligatur, sine operatione substantiam non esse in loco, nec transire de loco ad locum." Proposition 54-219: "Quod substantiae separatae nusquam sunt secundum substantiam.— Error, si intelligatur ita, quod substantia non sit in loco. Si autem intelligatur, quod substantia sit ratio essendi in loco, verum est, quod nusquam sunt secundum substantiam." For Godfrey's charge that condemned propositions 54 and 55 are in contradiction with one another, see his Quodlibet XII, q. 5, pp. 101-02. Cf. his remark concerning this a year later (1297/1298) in Quodlibet XIII, q. 4 (*Les philosophes Belges*, V, p. 221), where he refuses to decide the issue but notes that the condemned articles seem to be contrary to one another. Henry of Ghent had considerable difficulty in reconciling these same two condemned propositions in his Quodlibet II, q. 9 (pp. 66-

67) and acknowledges his perplexity in trying to determine the mind of the Bishop in condemning them both (see p. 68). According to Hissette, the views of Thomas and Albert, but more directly, those of Siger and Boethius of Dacia seem to be touched by these two propositions as well as by proposition 53-218: "Quod intelligentia, vel angelus, vel anima separata nusquam est." See *Enquête...*, pp. 104-10.

45. On proposition 1-40 see Hissette, *Enquête...*, pp. 15-18; Wippel, *Boethius of Dacia: On the Supreme Good, On the Eternity of the World, On Dreams* (Toronto, 1987), pp. 5-9. For the *De summo bono* see *Boethii Daci Opera: Opuscula ...*, N.G. Green-Pederson, ed. (Copenhagen, 1976), pp. 369-77. For the *De aeternitate mundi* see the same volume, p. 365:828-32. See Hissette, pp. 18-19. For a less sympathetic reading of Boethius on these points, see R.-A. Gauthier, "Notes sur Siger de Brabant: II. Siger en 1272-1275, Aubry de Reims et la scission des Normands," *Revue des Sciences philosophiques et théologiques* 68 (1984), pp. 19-20.

46. See Hissette, *Enquête ...*, pp. 274-75; Flasch, *Aufklärung ...*, pp. 217, 229-30. See A. Maurer, "Siger of Brabant on Fables and Falsehoods in Religion," *Mediaeval Studies* 43 (1981), pp. 515-30 for a helpful discussion of Siger's Commentary on Aristotle's views on the value of myths and on the role of fables in philosophy and religion. Maurer does not find any of these propositions defended by Siger himself.

47. Proposition 13-3 denies that God knows things other than himself, and proposition 14-56 asserts that God does not immediately know contingents except through particular and proximate causes. Proposition 15-42 would deny that God has knowledge of future contin-

gents and offers four arguments in support of this. On God's omnipotence see propositions 16 through 26 (Mandonnet numbering). Thus proposition 16-190 ("Quod Prima Causa est causa omnium remotissima.—Error, si intelligatur ita, quod non propinquissima") recalls the Neoplatonic-Avicennian doctrine of creation by way of intermediaries, and proposition 20-53 recalls the necessary emanation aspect of this same theory.

48. Propositions 21-39, 22-48, and 23-50 deny that God can produce something *de novo*, or produce a change in what he is moving. Propositions 25-72 and 26-29 restrict God's infinity to his ability to cause an infinite motion, or to his duration, thereby rejecting any notion of his intensive infinity. Proposition 27-34 denies that the First Cause can produce many worlds. This is one of two propositions singled out by P. Duhem as of greatest importance in breaking the dominant position held by Aristotelian physics at the time and thereby preparing the way for the development of a new physics in the fourteenth century and thereafter. The other proposition reads: "Quod Deus non possit movere caelum motu recto. Et ratio est, quia tunc relinqueret vacuum" (66-49). For a recent discussion and critique see J. Murdoch, "Pierre Duhem and the History of Late Medieval Science and Philosophy in the Latin West," in *Gli studi de filosofia medievale fra otto et novocento* (Rome, 1991), pp. 253-302, esp. pp. 259-62. For the claim that God can produce only one effect, see propositions 28-44 and 33-64.

49. On eternity of separate intelligences, see propositions 34-58, 38-70, 39-5, 40-80, 41-72. Eternity of the world is defended by a number, such as 80-91 (by

implication), 83-99, 84-98, 85-87, 87-4, 88-205, 89-
89 (by implication). Cyclical return of the same events
every 36,000 years is asserted by proposition 92-6. As
Hissette points out (*Enquête*, p.158), Tempier and his
censors may have had in mind a passage from Boethius
of Dacia's Commentary on the *Physics*, II, 25, but he
thinks it unlikely that Boethius accepted this as his
personal view.

50. On unicity of the human intellect see propositions
115-27 (one human soul), 117-32 (though the intellect is numerically one and may be separated from this
or that body, it will never be separated from every
body), 118-123 (unicity of the agent intellect, a position which, taken in itself, is perfectly orthodox), 120-
105 (that the form of a human being does not come
from without but is educed from the potency of
matter, thereby in effect denying its spirituality), 121-
11 (that a form coming from without cannot unite
with matter), 123-7 (that the intellect is not the form
of the body except in the way a sailor stands in relation
to a ship, and is not an essential perfection of a human
being). See propositions 125-119 and 126-121 on
how the separate intellect unites with the body (according to the second of these it is completely separate). For eternity of the human intellect and/or soul,
see propositions 129-109, 130-31, 131-125. For
propositions which appear to detract from human
freedom, see 151-194, 152-209, 153-133, 154-162,
155-132, 156-161, 157-208, 161-135, 162-173, 163-
163, 164-159, 165-158, 166-130. On this see the
eventual adoption by the Masters of Theology of the
propositio magistralis which opposes the condemnation of 166-130 ("Quod si ratio recta, et voluntas

recta.—Error quia ... "). See Hissette, *Enquête*, pp. 258ff., and R. Wielockx, *Aegidii Romani Opera Omnia* III.1 *Apologia* (Florence, 1985), pp. 105-09. See Godfrey's Quodlibet VIII, q. 16 (*Les Philosophes Belges*, Vol. 4, pp. 165-66), where he reasons that the articles rejected by Tempier must be interpreted in light of the *propositio magistralis*, not vice versa. Cf. Wielockx, *op.cit.*, pp. 77-80.

51. Efforts have been made to connect some of these, e.g., 205-183 and others with the *De deo amoris* of Andreas Capellanus which is explicitly mentioned by Tempier in the Prologue. See A. J. Denomy, "The *De Amore* of Andreas Capellanus and the Condemnation of 1277," *Mediaeval Studies* 8 (1946), esp. pp. 107-18, and for a review of recent discussion, R. Hissette, "Étienne Tempier et les menaces contre l'éthique chrétienne," *Bulletin de Philosophie médiévale* 21 (1979), pp. 68-72. While the spirit of free-love espoused in the first two books of Andreas's work is certainly rejected by Tempier's condemnation of these propositions, no direct textual connection has yet been established between the *De Amore* and these propositions. The naturalistic spirit expressed by proposition 200-177 is captured by some later thirteenth-century commentaries on the *Ethics* (by Giles of Orleans, and by anonymous authors) studied by R.-A. Gauthier, "Trois commentaires 'averroïstes' sur l'Éthique à Nicomaque," *Archives d'Histoire Doctrinale et Littéraire du Moyen Age* 16 (1947-1948), pp. 273-75, 277-95. Hissette (*Enquête*, p. 293) follows Gauthier in suggesting that a common source for these is probably prior to 1277 and envisioned by proposition 200-177.

52. Written sources for these have not been found.

53. See "Utrum humilitas sit virtus," in *Siger of Brabant. Écrits de logique, de morale et de physique*, B. Bazán, ed. (Louvain-Paris, 1974), pp. 98-99. Cf. Hissette, *Enquête* (pp. 301-02), who does not find Siger's position deserving of condemnation and notes that it is also defended by Aquinas in ST II-IIae, q. 161, a. 1, ad 1; a. 3.

54. See *Trois commentaires anonymes sur le Traité de l'âme d'Aristote*, M. Giele, F. Van Steenberghen, B. Bazán, eds. (Louvain-Paris, 1971), pp. 32-33.

55. For Gauthier's discussion see Leonine ed., Vol. 48, pp. B 49-B 55. For the text see p. B 126. Cf. ST II-IIae, q. 64, a. 5, ad 3 ("ultimum malorum huius vitae et maxime terribile est mors") where, when speaking in his own name, Thomas restricts this statement to the present life.

56. See already in the middle ages an attempt to classify the propositions according to a definite order undertaken by the unknown author of a *Collectio errorum in Anglia et Parisiis condemnatorum*, ed. by C. du Plessis d'Argentré, in *Collectio judiciorum de novis erroribus*, I (Paris, 1728), pp. 188-200. And see Mandonnet's systematic reordering as cited in n. 1 above and followed here. For Flasch see *Aufklärung ...*, pp. 55-56. He comments that the concept of order varies from age to age, and also that the mixture of chance and order present in the list was acceptable to Tempier. Bianchi credits Z. Kaluza for having called his attention to the fact that in the Introduction Tempier states that the condemned propositions were contained "in rotulo seu cedulis praesentibus his <litteris> annexo seu annexis." To Bianchi this suggests that the roll (*rotulus*) was nothing other than the sheets (*cedulae*) on which the various members of the Commission

had written the errors they had discovered. See *Il Vescovo*, p. 18. Wielockx (*Apologia*, pp. 14-15, and n. 41) finds a lack of systematic organization typical of censures of the period.

57. Cf. n. 44 above.

58. In addition to the *De deo amoris* of Andreas Capellanus, Tempier refers to a book of geomancy and gives the *incipit* and *explicit* (see Mandonnet ed., p. 176). On this see Hissette, "André le chapelain et la double vérité," in *Bulletin de Philosophie médiévale* 21 (1979), p. 63, n. 5.

59. For citation of this manuscript evidence see Mandonnet, *Siger de Brabant*, I, p. 220.

60. *Enquête*, p. 314. For the anonymous commentaries see P. Delhaye, ed., *Siger de Brabant. Questions sur la Physique d'Aristote. Texte inédit, Les Philosophes Belges*, Vol. 15 (Louvain, 1941); M. Giele, "Un commentaire averroïste sur les livres I et II du Traité de l'âme," in *Trois commentaires anonymes* (see n. 54), pp. 11-120; A. Zimmermann, ed., *Ein Kommentar zur Physik des Aristoteles aus der Pariser Artistenfakultät um 1273* (Berlin, 1968). Hissette agrees with Gauthier that one proposition is directed against the *Tabula* of the *Ethics* prepared for Aquinas by his secretary. Cf. n. 55 above.

61. *Enquête*, pp. 314-15.

62. See *Penser au Moyen Âge* (Paris, 1991), pp. 193-204. In fact, he writes: "En composant sa liste improbable, Étienne Tempier a, *autour du sexe*, donné corps à l'impalpable: il a inventé le projet philosophique du xiiie siècle" (p. 202).

63. See, for instance, Mandonnet, *Siger*, I, pp. 231-32, who suggests that some twenty attack more or less directly Aquinas's teaching, and p. 232, nn. 1-5, where he singles out fifteen; Gilson, *History of Chris-*

tian Philosophy, p. 406 and p. 728, n. 52 (where he repeats those listed by Mandonnet plus one, but notes that the list could be made longer or shorter); T. Crowley, "John Peckham, O.F.M., Archbishop of Canterbury, versus the new Aristotelianism," *Bulletin of the John Rylands Library* 33 (1950), p. 247 (nine were common to Thomas and Arts Masters); R. Zavalloni, *Richard de Mediavilla et la controverse sur la pluralité des formes* (Louvain, 1951), p. 217 (twenty more or less concern Thomas's doctrine); Wippel, *The Metaphysical Thought of Godfrey of Fontaines*, pp. 382-84 (on Godfrey's defense of Thomas from the Condemnation and his noting that a number of the condemned articles seem to be taken from Aquinas's writings); J. Weisheipl, *Friar Thomas Aquino*, 2nd pr. (Washington, D.C., 1983), pp. 336-37 (where he repeats the fifteen listed by Mandonnet plus proposition 55). In the early fourteenth century John of Naples discusses nine articles which were attributed to Thomas. See his Quodlibet VI, q. 2: "Quaestio Magistri Ioannis de Neapoli O. Pr. Utrum licite possit doceri Parisius doctrina fratris Thomae quantum ad omnes conclusiones eius hic primum in lucem edita," ed. by C. Jellouschek, *Xenia Thomistica*, III (Rome, 1925), pp. 73-104, text pp. 88-101.

64. See *Enquête*, pp. 315ff. For a more detailed defense of his interpretation see his "Albert le Grand et Thomas d'Aquin dans la censure Parisienne du 7 mars 1277," *Miscellanea Mediaevalia* 15 (1982), pp. 226-46. While he acknowledges that a number of Thomas's positions were touched by condemned propositions (p. 238), he continues to deny that Thomas was *directly* targeted (pp. 240, 241, 246).

65. In order to avoid acknowledging that proposition 213-178 directly envisions the *Tabula* of the *Ethics* drawn up under Aquinas's direction, Hissette offers a rather forced suggestion—that some Master of Arts had used it and that the passage was taken from this copy without the members of the Commission knowing its original source! (*Enquête*, pp. 306-07).

66. See *Aegidii Romani Opera Omnia III.1. Apologia*, pp. 49-59 (for the actual text); Ch. IV ("Date de la censure"), pp. 75-96.

67. *Op. cit.*, pp. 86-87, 92-99, 179, 215-19. For a fuller presentation of the evidence supporting a separate process against Aquinas, see Wielockx, "Autour du procès de Thomas d'Aquin," *Miscellanea Mediaevalia* 19 (1988), pp. 413-38. On the Oxford condemnations see D. Callus, *The Condemnation of St. Thomas at Oxford*, The Aquinas Society of London, Aquinas Paper, n. 5 (Oxford, 1946); Crowley, "John Peckham, O.F.M., Archbishop of Canterbury, versus the New Aristotelianism," pp. 242-55.

68. See *Expositio super librum Boethii De Trinitate*, B. Decker, ed. (Leiden, 1965), p. 94; also now available in Leonine ed., Vol. 50, pp. 98-99.

69. *Ibid.*

70. *Ibid.*

71. "Sicut enim ea quae sunt fidei non possunt demonstrative probari, ita quaedam contraria eis non possunt demonstrative ostendi esse falsa, sed potest ostendi ea non esse necessaria" (Decker ed., p. 94).

72. Decker ed., pp. 94-95.

73. For another explicit reference to reason's ability to demonstrate God's existence and unicity see SCG I, c. 3.

74. Leonine ed., Vol. 43, p. 314: "Adhuc autem gravius est quod postmodum dicit 'Per rationem concludo de necessitate quod intellectus est unus numero, firmiter tamen teneo oppositum per fidem'."

75. "... quod fidelium aures ferre non possunt" (*ibid.*).

76. Immediately before this statement Thomas also faults Siger for having presumed to dispute about matters of pure faith, such as whether the soul suffers from the fire of hell (*ibid.*).

77. For my own views on all of this, see my *Metaphysical Themes in Thomas Aquinas*, cc. 2, 3, and 4 on the nature of metaphysics and its subject, and c. 1 on "Thomas Aquinas and the Problem of Christian Philosophy." See especially pp. 22-33 on how one should go about recovering Thomas's philosophical thought from his many different kinds of texts.

78. One need only cite the letter sent by the Masters from the Arts Faculty at Paris on May 2, 1274, after they had heard of Aquinas's death, to the Dominican General Chapter meeting in Lyons. On this see V. Bourke, *Aquinas' Search for Wisdom* (Milwaukee, 1965), pp. 218-19; Weisheipl, *Friar Thomas d'Aquino*, pp. 332-33. Cf. *Chartularium*, I, pp. 504-05, n. 447.

79. For the dating see *Siger de Brabant. Écrits de logique, de morale et de physique*, B. Bazán, ed. (Louvain-Paris, 1974), p. 25. For Siger's solution see pp. 56-59.

80. Bazán ed., q. 2 ("Utrum intellectus sit aeternus vel de novo creatus") (p. 4). For his response see pp. 5-8. On Augustine vs. Aristotle see pp. 7:80-85, 8:96-99.

81. See *Siger de Brabant. Ecrits de logique ...*, *Impossibilia*, I, p. 73.

82. See Bazán ed., ch. 1 (pp. 116-17), the human species is held by the philosophers to be sempiternal; c. 2 (pp.

119-20), against arguments to prove that the human species began to be; c. 4 (p. 131), if the totality of being at some time did not exist, or if the human species began to be, potency would be prior to act, but both are impossible according to Aristotle.

83. See Bazán ed., Prologue (p. 70) for his intent in this treatise; c. 3 (pp. 83-84) for the rest. Note especially: "Sed nihil ad nos nunc de Dei miraculis, cum de naturalibus naturaliter disseramus." Cf. Albert the Great, *In de generatione et corruptione*, I, tr. 1, c. 22 (Cologne ed., Vol. 5.2, p. 129): "… dico, quod nihil ad me de dei miraculis, cum ego de naturalibus disseram."

84. *Ed. cit.*, pp. 92-93.

85. See *Siger de Brabant. Quaestiones in Metaphysicam*, A. Maurer, ed. (Louvain-la-Neuve, 1983), pp. 107-10 for the Cambridge version. Note especially: "Et credo quod, sicut ea quae fidei sunt per rationem humanam probari non possunt, ita sunt aliquae rationes humanae ad opposita eorum, quae per humanam rationem dissolvi non possunt" (p. 110:77-79). For the Paris version of this see Bk III, q. 5 (p. 412), where he counsels that one should not deny Catholic truth on account of some philosophical argument, even though one does not know how to resolve it (see lines 43-46).

86. See n. 71 above.

87. See *Avicenna Latinus. Liber de Philosophia Prima sive Scientia Divina V-X*, S. Van Riet, ed., with Intr. by G. Verbeke (Louvain-Leiden, 1980), pp. 481-84.

88. For Aquinas's knowledge of and refutation of this theory, see my "The Latin Avicenna as a Source for Thomas Aquinas's Metaphysics," *Freiburger Zeitschrift für Philosophie und Theologie* 37 (1990), pp. 76-90.

89. See J. J. Duin, *La doctrine de la providence dans les écrits de Siger de Brabant* (Louvain, 1954), pp. 19-24. For his qualifying expressions (*secundum intentionem philosophorum*) see pp. 19-20.

90. See Bazán ed., *Siger de Brabant. Écrits de logique ...*, pp. 112-113.

91. See, for instance, Duin, *La doctrine de la providence*, pp. 396-97, 417-18, 428-29; Bazán, *Écrits de logique ...*, pp. 30-32; Van Steenberghen, *Maître Siger*, pp. 313-15, who also finds Siger implicitly rejecting this view in q. 17 of his *Quaestiones in III De anima* (p. 64:94-97).

92. See Maurer ed., pp. 207-08.

93. See *Les quaestiones super librum de causis de Siger de Brabant*, A. Marlasca, ed. (Louvain-Paris, 1972), pp. 138-39.

94. Bazán ed., p. 3. In addition to the secondary sources cited above in n. 31, see E. P. Mahoney, "Saint Thomas and Siger of Brabant Revisited," *Review of Metaphysics* 27 (1974), pp. 531-53.

95. See q. 7 (p. 23), q. 8 (p. 25), and q. 9 (pp. 26-27) where he explicitly denies that the intellect is multiplied numerically in different human beings.

96. *Op. cit.*, p. 28. Siger turns to Averroes for reinforcement. "Et hoc intendens Averroes dicit quod intellectus speculativus iam ipse in omnibus est unus secundum recipiens, diversus autem secundum receptum." For Averroes see *In De anima* III, 5 (F. Stuart Crawford, ed. [Cambridge, Mass., 1953], p. 407).

97. See q. 13, pp. 44-45. Cf. q. 15 (p. 58:42-43). On Averroes's position see A. Hyman, "Aristotle's Theory of the Intellect and its Interpretation by Averroes," in *Studies in Aristotle*, D. J. O'Meara, ed. (Washington,

D.C., 1981), pp. 161-90, at pp. 183, 190; H. A. Davidson, *Alfarabi, Avicenna, and Averroes on Intellect* (New York-Oxford, 1992), especially pp. 292-93.

98. See Van Steenberghen, *Thomas Aquinas and Radical Aristotelianism*, pp. 51-53.

99. On this see B. Nardi, *Sigieri di Brabante nel pensiero del rinascimento italiano* (Rome, 1945), especially pp. 17-24, 46-47. Also see p. 24 for a text in which Nifo refers to still another lost work by Siger, his *Liber de felicitate*. See pp. 26ff.

100. Bazán ed., p. 70; and n. 83 above.

101. See pp. 81-82 (for Albert and Thomas); pp. 82-84 (for Siger's critique); pp. 85-86 (his effort to show that his interpretation can account for the fact that this individual human being may be said to understand). For Aquinas's charge that the Averroistic interpretation cannot account for this, see his *De unitate intellectus*, c. III (Leonine ed., Vol. 43, pp. 303-06).

102. Siger makes this observation in the midst of his critique of Albert, and adds the remark we have cited above in n. 83. See pp. 83-84. See p. 84:57-64 for Aristotle's position.

103. See p. 98, arg. 6.

104. *Ed. cit.*, p. 99. He adds that according to Aristotle rewards and punishments are due to the composite of soul and body and in this life are given by legislators who honor those who are virtuous and punish evildoers. He also suggests that the virtuous are rendered happy and the vicious are rendered miserable by their very works.

105. *Ed. cit.*, p. 100.

106. See p. 101. Note especially: "… quaerendo intentionem philosophorum in hoc magis quam veritatem,

cum philosophice procedamus." For discussion of this
seemingly curious way of defining philosophical research and its contrast with that of Aquinas, see Van
Steenberghen, *La philosophie* ..., pp. 344-45. Van
Steenberghen cites Aquinas (*De caelo* I, lect. 22), but
he also notes the similarity between Siger's approach
and that followed by Albert the Great in his Aristotelian Commentaries. Cf. above, n. 22.

107. See pp. 101-06 for his recapitulation of a series of
arguments against numerical multiplication of the
intellective soul in individual human beings. See p.
107 for his references to Avicenna, Algazel, and
Themistius, and his presentation of arguments in
support of numerical multiplication. For Aquinas's
rebuke and his citation of Themistius, Theophrastus
(indirectly as cited by Themistius), Avicenna, and Algazel
against the Averroistic reading, see *De unitate intellectus*,
c. II, especially p. 302 (Leonine ed., Vol. 43).

108. See p. 108:83-87.

109. See especially Mandonnet, *Siger de Brabant* ..., Vol.
1, pp. 132-36, 149-53, where he does mention Siger's
hesitations and protests of loyalty to the faith, but
appears to discount them, presumably because he sees
in the *De anima intellectiva* an important statement of
Siger's "Averroism." For an early more nuanced reading of Siger on this issue see F. Bruckmüller's inaugu-
ral dissertation, *Untersuchungen über Sigers (von
Brabant) Anima intellectiva* (Munich, 1908). For a
brief account of the controversy generated by this and
Mandonnet's harsh reaction, see Van Steenberghen,
Maître Siger ..., pp. 364-70. For another dismissal of
the importance of Siger's hesitations and protest of
faith in C. VII of the *De anima intellectiva*, also see

Mandonnet's "Autour de Siger de Brabant," *Revue thomiste* 19 (1911), pp. 500-02. For an overview of the *De anima intellectiva* also see Z. Kuksewicz, *De Siger de Brabant à Jacques de Plaisance* (Wroclaw-Varsovie-Cracovie, 1968), pp. 32-44. Also see Gilson, *History of Christian Philosophy in the Middle Ages* (New York, 1955), pp. 398-99, and his earlier remarks in his *Dante the Philosopher* (London, 1948), pp. 308-16, and 317-27 (concerning the discussion between Van Steenberghen and Nardi and the role of a set of *Quaestiones* on the *De anima* edited by Van Steenberghen in 1931 under Siger's name whose authenticity had been rightly questioned by Nardi).

110. See *Les Quaestiones super librum de causis de Siger de Brabant* (Louvain-Paris, 1972), A. Marlasca, ed. The editor dates them between 1274 and 1276 (see p. 29). Van Steenberghen prefers 1276 or, at the earliest, the 1275-1276 academic year (*Maître Siger* ..., p. 221). See q. 26, pp. 105-06. For Aquinas's *De unitate intellectus* see Leonine ed., Vol. 43, p. 307.

111. For Siger see *ed. cit.*, p. 106.

112. See pp. 111-12 for his exposition and rejection of the Averroistic position and pp. 112-13 for his own argument in support of numerical multiplication of human intellects.

113. See c. IV for this argumentation, especially p. 308 (Leonine ed.). As we have noted, in c. III Thomas had developed his case based on our consciousness that we ourselves, rather than some separate intellect, think or understand.

114. Interestingly, in commenting on Aquinas's accuracy in understanding Averroes's position on the intellect as presented in the latter's Long Commentary on the

De anima, Davidson notes that Thomas also takes him as denying that the intellect is the form of the body. Davidson notes that Averroes does not explicitly say this there; but he acknowledges that this view is probably implied by Averroes's defense of a single separate material (possible) intellect. See *Alfarabi, Avicenna, and Averroes ...,* p. 300.

115. For arguments against the eternity of the Intelligence, see p. 63. For those in support see pp. 63-66. For Siger's position see p. 66:89-94.

116. See *ed.cit.,* pp. 117-20.

117. See pr. 9-36: "Quod Deum in hac vita mortali possumus intelligere per essentiam;" pr. 10-215: "Quod de Deo non potest cognosci, nisi quia ipse est, sive ipsum esse." For Godfrey see Quodlibet XII, q. 5 (*Les Philosophes Belges* 5, p. 101): "Sed in istis videtur esse contradictio; quia inter cognitionem de aliquo quia est et quid est vel per essentiam medium non videtur." Also see his earlier Quodlibet VII, q. 5 (*Les Philosophes Belges* 3), p. 386. For Godfrey's own views on this issue see my *The Metaphysical Thought of Godfrey of Fontaines,* pp. 110-15.

118. For Siger's usual argumentation for God's existence see Van Steenberghen, *Maître Siger ...,* pp. 295-301. For the Munich manuscript of his *Quaestiones in Metaphysicam* see III, q. 1 (Dunphy ed., pp. 89-90). According to the testimony of Nipho, Siger also appears to defend this view in his *De intellectu* and especially so in his *De felicitate.* See Nardi, *Sigieri di Brabante ...,* p. 22 (*De intellectu*), p. 26, n. 1 (*De felicitate*); cf. Hissette, *Enquête ...,* pp. 31-32, and n. 7.

119. See *ed. cit.,* pp. 138-39. For Aquinas cf. *De potentia,* q. 3, a. 4; SCG II, c. 21; ST I, q. 45, a. 5. For more openness to the view that God could communicate to

a creature the power to create as an instrumental cause see *In II Sent.*, d. 1, q. 1, a. 3 (Mandonnet ed., Vol. 2), p. 22. For discussion see my "The Latin Avicenna as a Source for Thomas Aquinas's Metaphysics," *Freiburger Zeitschrift für Philosophie und Theologie* 37 (1990), pp. 78-79 and n. 58.

120. On these events see Van Steenberghen, *Maître Siger* ..., pp. 141-44, 21-27 (for a review of the evidence concerning Siger's final years), and c. IV, pp. 159-76 (where he attempts to sort out the few known facts from reasonable conjectures concerning additional details). Also see A. Zimmermann, "Dante hatte doch Recht. Neue Ergebnisse der Forschung über Siger von Brabant," *Philosophisches Jahrbuch* 75 (1967-1968), pp. 206-17; R.-A. Gauthier, "Notes sur Siger de Brabant. II. Siger en 1272-1275. Aubry de Reims et la scission des Normands," *Revue des Sciences philosophiques et théologiques* 68 (1984), pp. 25-28 (for a rather different interpretation); Van Steenberghen, *La philosophie au XIIIe siècle*, p. 339, n. 63 (critical reaction to Gauthier's remarks).

121. For an initial presentation of the discovery of these texts, see W. Dunphy and A. Maurer, "A Promising New Discovery for Sigerian Studies," *Mediaeval Studies* 29 (1967), pp. 364-69. The two versions of this discussion appear in the Vienna and Cambridge manuscripts of Siger's *Quaestiones in Metaphysicam* which, as we have seen, have been edited by Dunphy (Vienna) and by Maurer (Cambridge). The particular passages appear in the Dunphy edition at Bk VI, com. 1, pp. 359-61, and in the Maurer edition at Bk VI, q. 1, com., pp. 303:70-304:9. For Maurer's more recent comparison of Siger and Thomas on this, see his "Siger

of Brabant and Theology," *Mediaeval Studies* 50 (1988), pp. 257-78.

122. For Thomas see ST I, q. 1, a. 1, ad 2: "Unde theologia quae ad sacram doctrinam pertinet, differt secundum genus ab illa theologia quae pars philosophiae ponitur" (Leonine ed., Vol. 4, p. 7). For Siger see Cambridge version (Maurer ed., p. 303: 70-71: "Sed cum scientia ista, et etiam sacra scriptura, dicantur theologia, quaereret aliquis in quo differt haec ab illa;" Vienna version (Dunphy ed., p. 359:4-7): "Consequenter quaeritur qualiter differat scientia theologia quam prae manibus habemus, quae est pars philosophiae, et scientia theologia quae non est pars philosophiae sed est sacra scriptura, nam utraque dicitur theologia." On the science of being as being see Cambridge version, p. 303: 63-66 (and earlier in q. 1, pp. 300-01); Vienna version, pp. 358-59.

123. See Cambridge version (Maurer ed., p. 303:73-76); Vienna version (Dunphy ed., pp. 359:16-360:26). Cf. ST I, q. 1, a. 8, ad 2.

124. See Cambridge version (Maurer ed., p. 304:77-84); Vienna version (Dunphy ed., p. 360:27-39).

125. Cambridge version (Maurer ed., p. 304:85-91); Vienna version (Dunphy ed., p. 360: 40-47).

126. Cambridge version (Maurer ed., p. 304: 92-97). This appears as the fifth difference in the Vienna version (Dunphy ed., p. 361:61-74).

127. Cambridge version (Maurer ed., p. 304:98-103). In the Vienna version this appears as the fourth difference (Dunphy ed., p. 360:48-p. 361:60). For Thomas see his *De unitate intellectus* as cited above in n. 74. Also see above for Siger's acknowledgment in the Cambridge version at Bk III, q. 15 that certain argu-

ments for positions opposed to the faith cannot be resolved by human reason (see n. 85 above and our corresponding text).

128. Cambridge version (Maurer ed., p. 304:104-09); Vienna version (Dunphy ed., p. 361:75-87).

129. This appears only in the Vienna version (Dunphy ed., p. 361:88-93).

130. See n. 127 above.

131. In addition to my remarks above, cf. Van Steenberghen, *Maître Siger* ..., pp. 232-57, and Maurer, "Siger of Brabant and Theology," pp. 268-74.

132. See T. B. Bukowski, "Siger of Brabant vs. Thomas Aquinas on Theology," *The New Scholasticism* 61 (1987), pp. 25-32, and "Siger of Brabant, Anti-Theologian," *Franciscan Studies* 50 (1990), pp. 57-82. Maurer responded to the first of these in his 1988 article in *Mediaeval Studies* ("Siger of Brabant and Theology"), and Bukowski replies to Maurer's response in his 1990 article.

133. For references to these secondary sources see Maurer, "Siger of Brabant and Theology," p. 258. Also see P.E. Persson, *Sacra Doctrina. Reason and Revelation in Aquinas* (Philadelphia, 1970), pp. 86-87. Note Persson's citation there from ST I, q. 1, a. 3 (n. 63), and from ST I, q. 1, a. 2, ad 2, about which he comments: "Scripture and theology are here declared to be synonymous terms" (p. 86). For Thomas's Commentary on the *De Trinitate* see Decker ed., p. 87, especially lines 7-21. For Siger see n. 123 above.

134. Decker ed., p. 195, especially lines 10-11, 24-25.

135. See *Summa theologiae (Summa de mirabili scientia Dei: Prima Pars)*, Tr. I, q. 3, c. 1 (Cologne ed., Vol. 34, pp. 10-11; c. 2, p. 12; c. 3, p. 13).

136. For more on his life and works see my *Boethius of Dacia. On the Supreme Good. On the Eternity of the World. On Dreams* (Toronto, 1987), pp. 1-5.

137. Critical editions of Boethius's works have appeared in the series *Corpus Philosophorum Danicorum Medii Aevi*, as *Boethii Daci Opera*. For our purposes see Vol. VI, Pars II: *Opuscula: De aeternitate mundi-De summo bono-De somniis*, N. G. Green-Pedersen, ed. (Copenhagen, 1976). See pp. 369-71.

138. *Ed. cit.*, pp. 371-72, especially p. 372:75-78. For English see Wippel tr. (as cited in n. 136 above), p. 29.

139. *Ed. cit.*, pp. 373-74 (on the small number of human beings who actually pursue the true supreme good and true happiness); pp. 374-77 (on the rightness and happiness of the life of the philosopher). See p. 377:239-42 (for his "definition" of the philosopher). See Wippel translation, p. 35, for text cited in English.

140. For a very critical interpretation see Mandonnet, "Note complémentaire sur Boèce de Dacie," *Revue des Sciences philosophiques et théologiques* 22 (1933), p. 250. For a more balanced but still critical evaluation see Gauthier, "Notes sur Siger de Brabant: II ...," p. 20. For more sympathetic interpretations see Van Steenberghen, *La philosophie au XIIIe siècle*, p. 362; Hissette, *Enquête ...*, pp. 17-18; also A. H. Celano, "Boethius of Dacia: 'On the Highest Good'," *Traditio* 43 (1987), pp. 199-214, for a somewhat different but still sympathetic reading.

141. Cf. Wippel, *Boethius of Dacia ...*, pp. 7-9. For Henry see his *Summa quaestionum ordinariarum* (Paris, 1520), a. 7, q. 10, f. 60rBC. Note especially: "... qui philosophicis diligit insistere propter se non potest, vel vix potest errores evadere verae fidei contrarios. ...

Unde in scientiis liberalibus stare propter delectationem illius scire quod in eis invenitur, non ordinando scire acquisitum ex illis ad aliam utilitatem, et maxime in usum huius scientiae (i.e., theology), omnino illicitum est." Cited and interpreted by S. F. Brown, "Henry of Ghent's 'De reductione artium ad theologiam'," in *Thomas Aquinas and his Legacy*, D. M. Gallagher, ed. (Washington, D.C., 1994), pp. 203-04.

142. See Green-Pedersen ed., p. 335:1-8.

143. *Ed. cit.*, pp. 335:9-336:27. This opening section, consisting of 27 lines in the critical edition, is well worth reading in its entirety. For an English rendering see my *Boethius of Dacia* :..., pp. 36-37.

144. *Ed. cit.*, pp. 336:28-338:95 (arguments against eternity of the world); pp. 339:99-340:134 (arguments for possibility of an eternal world); pp. 340:140-346:308 (arguments for an eternal world).

145. Compare this condemned proposition with Boethius's text, *ed. cit.*, p. 347:314-322. As Hissette has pointed out (*Enquête*, pp. 24-25), Boethius makes the same point at p. 355:548-551, and in another work, his *Questions on the Physics* I, q. 2a (ed. by G. Sajó, *Opera omnia*, V. 2, p. 140:25-28). But the parallel with the condemned proposition is closest in the first text cited here.

146. For Aristotle see *Metaphysics* IV, c. 2 (1004a 2-9); and *Metaphysics* VI, c. 1, *passim*. For Boethius see *ed. cit.*, p. 347:321-332.

147. *Ed. cit.*, pp. 347:333-348:339. Boethius also comments that in his *Physics* Aristotle did not begin with the First Principle in the absolute sense, but with the first principle for natural things, scil., prime matter, which he identifies as nature in Bk II (see lines 339-43).

148. *Ed. cit.*, pp. 348:345-350:398.

149. *Ed. cit.*, pp. 350:399-351:420.

150. See p. 351:421-437.

151. *Ed. cit.*, pp. 351:438-352:455.

152. On the mathematician see pp. 353:493-354:530; on the metaphysician see pp. 354:531-355:547. On Thomas Aquinas's views on the possibility of demonstrating that the world began to be (which he always denied) and the possibility of an eternal world (which he finally explicitly defended in his *De aeternitate mundi*) see my *Metaphysical Themes in Thomas Aquinas* ..., Ch. 8. For the different positions of Aquinas and Bonaventure on the general issue see Van Steenberghen, *Thomas Aquinas and Radical Aristotelianism*, pp. 9-18. For Henry of Ghent see Quodlibet I, qq. 7-8 of 1276, and R. Macken, "La temporalité radicale de la créature selon Henri de Gand," *Recherches de Théologie ancienne et médiévale* 38 (1971), pp. 211-72. And now see two more general studies: L. Bianchi, *L'errore di Aristotele. La polemica contro l'eternità del mondo nel XIII secolo* (Florence, 1984); R. C. Dales, *Medieval Discussions of the Eternity of the World* (Leiden, 1990). Dales accepts the view recently proposed by S. Baldner to the effect that Bonaventure did not explicitly maintain that the noneternity of the world can be demonstrated (pp. 86, 128), while recognizing that this is not the common reading of Bonaventure. For Baldner see "St. Bonaventure on the Temporal Beginning of the World," *The New Scholasticism* 63 (1989), pp. 206-28.

153. For his refutation of arguments in support of eternity of the world, see pp. 357:594-364:802. As for the arguments against eternity of the world, he grants

them "for the sake of the conclusion, although they can be resolved, since they are sophistical" (p. 364:803-804). He does not reply to the arguments he had offered in support of the possibility of an eternal world, presumably because he grants this. See pp. 364:805-365:848 for his insistence that there is no real contradiction between faith and the philosopher concerning this and similar topics since the philosopher maintains that things are possible or not possible through arguments subject to rational investigation and according to natural causes.

154. See p. 352:457-65. For recent discussions of the presence or absence of a double-truth theory in Boethius, see Van Steenberghen, *Thomas Aquinas and Radical Aristotelianism*, pp. 95-99; Bianchi, *Il Vescovo ...*, p. 113 and n. 27 (for additional references).

155. See pp. 352:466-353:490. Cf. p. 364:805 to end of the treatise.

156. See p. 366:848-857.

157. See Hissette, *Enquête...*, pp. 314-15, for a summary of his findings concerning this.

158. See D. Callus, *The Condemnation of St. Thomas at Oxford*, The Aquinas Society of London (Oxford, 1946); R. Zavalloni, *Richard de Mediavilla et la controverse sur la pluralité des formes* (Louvain, 1951), pp. 218-21.

159. For William's *Correctorium* along with a refutation by Richard Knapwell, see P. Glorieux, *Les premières polémiques thomistes: I. Le Correctorium Corruptorii "Quare"* (Le Saulchoir, Kain, 1927). On this and the five Dominican responses which have been edited, see J.-P. Torrell, *Initiation à saint Thomas d'Aquin. Sa personne et son œuvre* (Fribourg, 1993), pp. 446-50;

M. Jordan, "The Controversy of the *Correctoria* and the Limits of Metaphysics," *Speculum* 57 (1982), pp. 292-314.

160. See note 141 above and the study by Brown cited there.

161. Wippel, *The Metaphysical Thought of Godfrey* ..., pp. 381-82. For a helpful presentation of defenders and critics of Aquinas during this period, see P. Glorieux, "Pro et contra Thomam. Un survol de cinquante années," in *Sapientiae Procerum Amore, Studia Anselmiana* 63 (Rome, 1974), pp. 255-87.

The Aquinas Lectures
Published by the Marquette University Press
Milwaukee WI 53233 USA

1. *St. Thomas and the Life of Learning.* JOHN F. McCORMICK, S.J. (1937) 0-87462-101-1

2. *St. Thomas and the Gentiles.* MORTIMER J. ADLER (1938) 0-87462-102-X

3. *St. Thomas and the Greeks.* ANTON C. PEGIS (1939) 0-87462-103-8

4. *The Nature and Functions of Authority.* YVES SIMON (1940) 0-87462-104-6

5. *St. Thomas and Analogy.* GERALD B. PHELAN (1941) 0-87462-105-4

6. *St. Thomas and the Problem of Evil.* JACQUES MARITAIN (1942) 0-87462-106-2

7. *Humanism and Theology.* WERNER JAEGER (1943) 0-87462-107-0

8. *The Nature and Origins of Scientism.* JOHN WELLMUTH (1944) 0-87462-108-9

9. *Cicero in the Courtroom of St. Thomas Aquinas.* E.K. RAND (1945) 0-87462-109-7

10. *St. Thomas and Epistemology.* LOUIS-MARIE REGIS, O.P. (1946) 0-87462-110-0

11. *St. Thomas and the Greek Moralists.* VERNON J. BOURKE (1947)
0-87462-111-9

12. *History of Philosophy and Philosophical Education.* ÉTIENNE GILSON (1947) 0-87462-112-7

13. *The Natural Desire for God.* WILLIAM R. O'CONNOR (1948)
0-87462-113-5

14. *St. Thomas and the World State.* ROBERT M. HUTCHINS (1949)
0-87462-114-3

15. *Method in Metaphysics.* ROBERT J. HENLE, S.J. (1950)
0-87462-115-1

16. *Wisdom and Love in St. Thomas Aquinas.* ÉTIENNE GILSON (1951) 0-87462-116-X

17. *The Good in Existential Metaphysics.* ELIZABETH G. SALMON (1952) 0-87462-117-8

18. *St. Thomas and the Object of Geometry.* VINCENT E. SMITH (1953) 0-87462-118-6

19. *Realism And Nominalism Revisted.* HENRY VEATCH (1954)
0-87462-119-4

20. *Imprudence in St. Thomas Aquinas.* CHARLES J. O'NEIL (1955) 0-87462-120-8

21. *The Truth That Frees.* GERARD SMITH, S.J. (1956)
0-87462-121-6

22. *St. Thomas and the Future of Metaphysics.* JOSEPH OWENS, C.Ss.R. (1957) 0-87462-122-4

48. *The Reality of the Historical Past.* PAUL RICOEUR (1984)
 0-87462-152-6

49. *Human Ends and Human Actions: An Exploration in St. Thomas' Treatment.* ALAN DONAGAN (1985)   0-87462-153-4

50. *Imagination and Metaphysics in St. Augustine.* ROBERT O'CONNELL, S.J. (1986)   0-87462-227-1

51. *Expectations of Immortality in Late Antiquity.* HILARY A. ARMSTRONG (1987)   0-87462-154-2

52. *The Self.* ANTHONY KENNY (1988)   0-87462-155-0

53. *The Nature of Philosophical Inquiry.* QUENTIN LAUER, S.J. (1989)   0-87562-156-9

54. *First Principles, Final Ends and Contemporary Philosophical Issues.* ALASDAIR MACINTYRE (1990)   0-87462-157-7

55. *Descartes among the Scholastics.* MARJORIE GRENE (1991)
 0-87462-158-5

56. *The Inference That Makes Science.* ERNAN MCMULLIN (1992)
 0-87462-159-3

57. *Person and Being.* W. NORRIS CLARKE, S.J. (1993)
 0-87462-160-7

58. *Metaphysics and Culture.* LOUIS DUPRÉ (1994)
 0-87462-161-5

59. *Mediæval Reactions to the Encounters between Faith and Reason.* JOHN F. WIPPEL (1995)   0-87462-162-3

The Annual St. Thomas Aquinas Lecture Series began at Marquette University in the Spring of 1937. Ideal for classroom use, library additions, or private collections, the Aquinas Series has received international acceptance by scholars, universities, and libraries. Hardbound in maroon cloth with gold stamped covers. Some reprints with soft covers. Complete set (59 Titles) (ISBN 0-87462-150-X $354 (= 40% discount; $590 if purchased separately). Uniform style and price ($10 Each). New standing orders receive a 30% discount. Shipping on standing orders is only $1. Regular reprinting keeps all volumes available.

Ordering information:
Purchase orders, checks, and major credit cards accepted (Visa, Master Card, Discover, American Express).

Marquette University Press
1313 W. Wisconsin Ave.
Milwaukee WI 53233
Phone: 414-288-1564   Fax: 414-288-3300

Credit card orders and other subscription communications may also be sent via the Internet to
BergerM@VMS.CSD.MU.EDU
and via CompuServe email to Andy Tallon, 73627,1125.

ISBN 0-87462-162-3

9 780874 621624